FORGOTTEN RAILWAYS

Volume 10

The West Midlands

THE FORGOTTEN RAILWAYS SERIES

Edited by Allan Patmore

Others are in preparation

BY THE SAME AUTHOR

Forgotten Railways
Volume 4   *North and Mid Wales*

A Regional History of the Railways of Great Britain
Volume 7   *The West Midlands*
Volume 13   *Thames & Severn*

FORGOTTEN RAILWAYS
Volume 10

The West Midlands

REX CHRISTIANSEN

DAVID ST JOHN THOMAS
DAVID & CHARLES

British Library Cataloguing in Publication Data

Christiansen, Rex
  The West Midlands.—(Forgotten railways; v. 10)
  1. Railroads—England—Midlands—
  Abandonment
  I. Title II. Series
  385'.09424 HE3019.W/

  ISBN 0–946537–01–1

Photoset in 11/13 Baskerville
and printed in Great Britain
by Redwood Burn Ltd Trowbridge
for David St John Thomas
Distributed by David & Charles (Holdings) Ltd
Brunel House Newton Abbot Devon
Published in the United States of America
by David & Charles Inc
North Pomfret Vermont 05053 USA

Contents

Note The description of an old railway route does not imply that there is a public right of way, and readers must obtain permission to enter private land.

List of Plates

Jacket illustration Perhaps the platform most missed in the whole of the West Midlands is that on which people waited for trains on the other route to London. Here, on 18 August 1962, No 6002 *King William IV* is seen heading a Birkenhead to Paddington express at Birmingham Snow Hill. This was only a month before the Kings, based at Wolverhampton Stafford Road, were withdrawn from regular service, though such was the unreliability of the early diesels that five Kings were steamed every day for some weeks to cover failures. The airiness of Snow Hill contrasted with the noisy, almost subterranean world of New Street. (*Photograph B. J. Ashworth*)

CHAPTER 1

Keeping Memory Green

Clockwork springs of delight

Discovering from an airport photograph taken on landing at Las Palmas that I had a balding patch I had not seen before, I had to accept, with regret, the arrival of middle age. But I quickly consoled myself with the thought that if I had not now been in my fifties, I would not have known the working days of some of the lines about which I am to write with enthusiasm and nostalgia.

Nor, perhaps, would I have ever known the joy of getting a boxed train set and sending a Hornby gauge O tank whizzing around tinplate track and waiting until its motor began to wind down and it was running slow enough for me to switch the points for tank and trucks to run in and out of a short loop; a loop which, in boyish eyes, was sufficient to boost the status of the layout from that of the very basic large circle almost to that of a busy main line.

Today, I find the little station at Old Hill a sad place, partly because it is no longer the junction for Halesowen and Dudley, but Old Hill is in my mind whenever I recall my first Hornby, for it is likely (though I shall never know for certain) that its clockwork motor, which I wound with a large key, was made there. The High Haden works of C & G Gauges Ltd produced

9

clockwork motors by the million each year for model cars, boats, novelty toys and all types of O and OO train sets.

In 1985, the GWR 150th anniversary year, it is sad to remember that the most important forgotten railway in the West Midlands once belonged to that proud company: the 12½ mile main line between Birmingham (Snow Hill) and Wolverhampton (Low Level). But it is pleasing to report that part of the trackbed is soon to come to life again as part of the second Birmingham Cross-City Line between the commuter areas to the south, and Kidderminster, a town which since a glorious summer's day in 1984 has revelled in the glories of re-stored Great Western steam, as the new terminus of the pre-served Severn Valley Railway.

The Snow Hill Cross-City station of tomorrow will lie hidden beneath tall office blocks and bear no resemblance to its predecessor, which had the power in life, and for a time after death, to excite the imagination and memories of thousands of railway buffs. But passengers often hated it because, despite its elegance, pleasant buildings, wide platforms and layout, it was a place where they queued for hours: a night-mare curtain-raiser to holidays in Devon and Cornwall. Snow Hill must surely have looked drab and foreboding even on the brightest of summer dawns. Today's holidaymakers, stuck in long queues on the M5 in the West Country, at least have more pleasant scenery to enjoy.

Wolverhampton, which has lost several lines and passenger services, was always a tremendously restrictive frontier in GWR history. It was as far north as the broad gauge ever went, the dream of it reaching the Mersey at Birkenhead being shattered at junctions north of Low Level station. For years Wolverhampton was also the most northerly town to which King class locomotives were allowed to run. Their operating limit was Oxley North, Middle and Branch Junctions with the Wombourn branch. They turned on this triangle when the Stafford Road locomotive shed turntable was busy. Then, for a short but heady period in the early 1960s, towards the end of their reign, the ban was relaxed and the Kings strode across the Shropshire countryside to Shrewsbury, the Cambrian Coast Express being a notable turn.

Wolverhampton's Stafford Road works lacked the glamour of Swindon, but they provided satisfying moments for enthusiasts for they were the place to which a variety of elderly engines, from Dean 0–6–0s to the 2–4–0 tanks which haunted the Welsh Marches for years, gathered for rest and repair. And that meant they could be examined in comfort during society visits.

Only railwaymen knew of Wolverhampton's role as the final resting place of old records from the company's Northern Division. They were sent there by officials obeying page 299 of the General Appendix to the Rule Book:

> Old books, papers, etc., at every station must be overhauled annually and those over age forwarded to the Stores Department, application being made to the Storekeeper for the necessary sacks...

Dudley has been without a passenger service for years, although its name is back on the railway map as 'Sandwell & Dudley', opened in 1984 on the site of the former Oldbury station and goods yard.

While the northern tip of the Oxford Worcester & Wolverhampton, threading the industrial areas between Dudley and Wolverhampton, continues to sink into oblivion, the rural southern end has become the successful 'Cotswold Line', which has put fresh transport heart into that glorious countryside.

But there is no prospect for the revival of the short, once intensively worked goods branches in the Stourbridge area. Geoffrey Bannister, who has recorded the West Midland railway scene for many years, volunteered to search for them. He returned to his home beside the former Wombourn (GWR spelling) branch and wrote:

> I was quite shocked at the speed at which 'evidence on the ground' disappears, because apart from the terminus of the Spinners End branch, it requires a vivid imagination to realise that any of these

lines ever existed. There is no fossilisation here in the Black Country, unlike the Manchester & Milford Railway from Penponbren Junction to Llangurig which my son and I investigated last week!

I stayed in Stourbridge while researching lines to Halesowen. Future generations are likely to find few relics of those either. Most traces have gone as surely as the wake of passing boats on the local canal.

Interchange basins for canal and rail traffic were important features of the West Midlands transport arteries, and railways, especially, made great efforts to develop them. The Halesowen railway builders went down a gradient of 1 in 38 to their basin. And for years drivers who received the red wooden train-staff were faced with a tricky job.

The line from Halesowen over the hill to Longbridge was through rolling countryside and you can still enjoy its delights if you go in search of the route today. The most satisfying stretch is to be found just north of the M5.

While the old GWR system has suffered grievously, that of the London & North Western has remained virtually intact, and the restored, award-winning Curzon Street station building (albeit no longer in railway use) is a reminder of the dignity of the London & Birmingham Railway and, more poignantly, of what London has lost through the destruction of the Euston Arch.

Casualties suffered by the LNWR in the Black Country are notable for having occurred in very recent years. They include the Princes End branch.

Of the areas with heavy concentrations of industry, that which has suffered least is Coventry. While it lost its avoiding line as the patterns of industry and transport of its products, including cars, changed, it has seen the re-opening to passengers of the mainly single line to Leamington Spa.

The former Midland system may suffer further as I write for the Whitacre Loop off the Birmingham–Derby main line is under threat. But the main line's future is not in doubt, though it has been slimmed down, notably through the closure of local stations on both sides of Birmingham (New Street), and the run-down of Washwood Heath marshalling yards, where once I saw LMS Garratts, looking lazy and lumbering and fascinating.

Creation of the Birmingham Cross-City Line from Longbridge to Four Oaks brought about the revival of several former Midland stations, while those on the Direct Line, Camp Hill among them, are unlikely candidates for reopening, not least because the line runs across the grain of roads in and out of the city centre. But some services between Birmingham (New Street) and Worcester circle the city centre, using the Cross-City route inward, and the Direct Line outward.

If you want to walk old railways in profusion, North Staffordshire can oblige (well, almost); for while this is a Region where much of the heart has been torn out of railways, it is also one where their remains have been put to practical and pleasant use.

There was good precedent, for after the London Midland & Scottish Railway closed the narrow-gauge Leek & Manifold Light Railway in 1935, it presented the trackbed to Staffordshire County Council which converted it into a walkway, which was admirable, but one which was laid with a hard surface. That reminded ramblers, who arrived to get away from town and city cares, of pavements and home. There was no spring in the turf. But the hills were sufficiently enticing to make the valley attractive to visitors until, in the '80s, it is almost under siege at times.

It is not quite so easy, indeed it is almost impossible, to get away from the urban scene on the Loop Line Greenway moulded from the Potteries Loop, but it is pleasant. Successors to Arnold Bennett's role as an affectionate portrayer of the line, are the authors of a booklet prepared by the City of Stoke-on-Trent, and people who sing its praises from time to time. H. C. Hopkinson wrote to the *Railway Magazine* in October 1976 to say: 'It is certainly not as most people would imagine a backyard view of smoky chimneys, but it is in fact quite a scenic pathway...'

A miniature steam railway based on the Leek & Manifold had a short life on the trackbed of the Churnet Valley line beside Rudyard Lake. Standard-gauge enthusiasts tried to establish a line between the lake and Leek and, when frustrated, moved deeper into the valley, centring their activities on the mock Tudor station at Cheddleton. Steam revival continues in part of the valley known as 'Staffordshire's Little Switzerland'.

Part of the Churnet Valley line has been incorporated into the Staffordshire Way walking route, while close to the heart of Birmingham is a much shorter venture: the Harborne Line Walkway Nature Trail. I arrived to explore it at about 6 o'clock on a spring evening when, once upon a time, city businessmen would have been returning home on the short LNWR trains, which puffed through the trees and along a high embankment at the approach to the terminus.

Miles of disused lines are to be found in the West Midlands. More and more sections are being developed for public use, to provide more breathing spaces.

Let the last introductory words go to Geoff Allen who wrote, in his 'Out Walking' column in the *Birmingham Evening Mail* of 29 November 1980, in praise of the Halesowen–Frankley route:

> I am fascinated by disused railway lines. I class them with stone circles, burial mounds, ruined castles and old green lanes for antiquarian interest.

CHAPTER 2

Birmingham: GWR

Decimated main line

What a magnificent station Snow Hill was!

> The platform accommodation ranks second only to Paddington
> throughout the Great Western system. Each of the four main through
> platforms is approximately 1,200ft long, capable of taking 16 or 17 of
> the longest coaches with engine ... The platform and signalling
> arrangements are such as to give the maximum scope for dealing with
> our famous two-hour Birmingham and Paddington expresses, and
> the local trains connecting therewith.

The quotation is from a speech by the Assistant Divisional
Superintendent, Birmingham, J. W. Enser, to the Great Western Railway (London) Lecture and Debating Society at the
General Meeting Room at Paddington on a January evening
in 1931, starting 'promptly at 5.45pm'.

More than half a century later, Snow Hill still makes history
in the GWR's 150th anniversary year—as the largest demolished station in the West Midlands. But soon it will have
no place, officially, in a 'Forgotten Railways' volume. For beneath the tall office and shopping blocks arising on its site in
1984 lay the embryo of a new station for a second Birmingham
Cross-City Line, from the commuter areas south of the city to
Kidderminster.

It was the Great Western's hub in the West Midlands: there was no other comparable focal point. It was opened in 1852 when the mixed-gauge Birmingham & Oxford was completed, two years ahead of the Birmingham Wolverhampton & Dudley, authorised at the same time in August 1846.

The year 1852 was also important for the LNWR, with the formal opening of New Street station, knitting together the passenger services of trunk routes which other companies built into the West Midlands years ahead of the GWR: the Grand Junction (1837), London & Birmingham (1838), Birmingham and Gloucester (1841) and Birmingham & Derby Junction (1842), the latter two providing the Midland with a magnificent north-east–south-west through route.

Initially, the four underground platforms of the new Snow Hill will be the terminus of trains from Stratford-upon-Avon and Leamington Spa. They will call at a second projected station: a Moor Street station with through lines, which will be built at the southern mouth of Snow Hill tunnel. This will come to life again as part of the new Cross-City line.

Snow Hill was always unmistakably the station of a great city, while Moor Street, which the new station will replace, remains vaguely rural in character, a gem, with a small concourse, low roof and modest buildings (flower baskets, too, and friendly staff, when I was last there). No station I know that is dominated by tall buildings seems so remote from its city and the life outside.

Moor Street station was an important Edwardian addition to the Birmingham railway scene being opened in 1909 as the city expanded and people discovered that the leafy areas of Warwickshire were the places to live. It became the terminus for the Birmingham & North Warwickshire line and gave 'much relief', in the words of a GWR official, to Snow Hill. Many summer holiday specials to the West of England and South Wales were handled at Moor Street, partly because it had spare capacity as its suburban services from Leamington Spa and Stratford-upon-Avon never grew to the volume hoped, and suffered severely from bus competition.

THE END OF A NAMED EXPRESS BEFORE THAT OF A STATION: *Plate 1 (above)* The Cornishman arrives at Snow Hill, Birmingham, on its last journey to the West of England, 7 September 1962. 'Castle' No 7001 *Sir James Milne; Plate 2 (below)* notable for its longevity for goods: Henley-in-Arden Old Station. Closed to passengers when the Birmingham & North Warwickshire line opened in 1908, it survived for goods until 31 December 1962. Photographed 9 January 1962.

BIRMINGHAM LNWR: *Plate 3 (above)* Edwardian Harborne. Stopping train arriving from Birmingham (New Street), hauled by Webb 2–4–2 tank. 1906. The Harborne branch was notable as one of only a few which the LNWR developed in the Birmingham area; *Plate 4 (below)* Handsworth Wood station was built to serve suburbs never built. Soho Road, also closed 5 May 1941, was the only other station on the now-electrified Soho Loop.

When Moor Street is replaced, the Great Western's presence in Birmingham city centre will ebb further away. Among the most evocative places remaining will be St Chad's Circus and the mural inside the pedestrian area depicting five phases of the history of Snow Hill station. Unveiled in 1969, when the station was, of course, still in use, it is ever refreshing and enjoyable to visit.

The Birmingham Wolverhampton & Dudley trackbed cuts a wide route north from Snow Hill towards Hockley, where the goods depot, now demolished for industrial development, was one of the GWR's biggest in the Birmingham area. It was connected by pilot line, independent of the main line, to Soho & Winson Green goods yard, $\frac{3}{4}$ mile further north. The yard finally closed in November 1971 and after site clearance with government financial aid, West Midlands County Council began development of a 7 acre business park in partnership with a private development company. Construction work began in July 1984.

The Soho & Winson Green yard lay under the shadow of the LNWR Soho Loop. Now electrified, the Loop gives passengers of emus or diverted expresses grandstand views of a short section of the BW & D that is very much alive. It runs to the Handsworth & Smethwick cement terminal at Queen's Head sidings. It handles merry-go-round trains using the now singled section from Handsworth Junction, again projected as part of the second Cross-City route.

Immediately north of Handsworth & Smethwick station site, the Wolverhampton line was flanked by the extensive works of the Birmingham Railway Carriage & Wagon Company. They closed in the mid 1960s, making several thousand workers redundant, a reminder that casualties of rationalisation and contraction have not been confined to British Rail.

The GWR and Western Region propelled wagons into the works from Handsworth & Smethwick goods yard. Their closures consigned to history Sectional Appendix instructions such as:

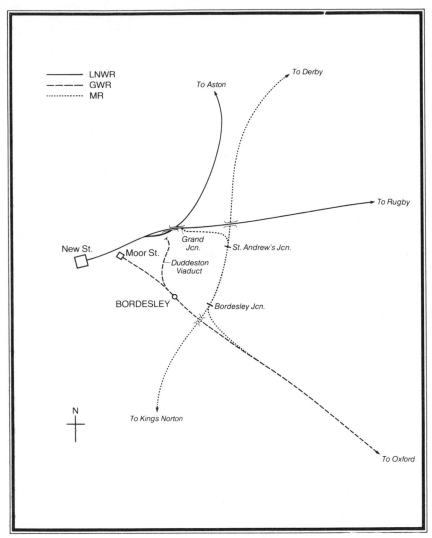

Duddeston Viaduct. Its purpose to link the LNWR and GWR was eventually achieved by the Midland! It built what is now an Inter City route between Grand Junction and Bordesley Junction. Duddeston Viaduct is gradually being cleared: demolition of a further section began in April 1985

Enginemen must not propel the wagons at a greater speed than 4 miles per hour, and they must be prepared to stop at once if the Signal is given by the Shunter. The Engine whistle must be sounded at intervals, and the Shunters are strictly forbidden to ride in the wagons.

Life in the neighbourhood has been quieter since railways departed.

The local landscape which the railway helped to shape in Victorian times has been remoulded, not least through the creation of the Middlemoor Industrial Estate on the works site. Small firms are housed in buildings old and new in a spacious layout, where the atmosphere is far less factory, far less oppressive, than in the long buildings of the original works.

One of the many outstanding products of those works, and a satisfying testimony to the workers' skills, is to be found in the National Railway Museum, where the Pullman parlour car, *Topaz*, is the only traditional-built Pullman in the national collection. It is pleasant simply to stand dwarfed beneath the shapely car and admire not only the car itself, but the restoration work that has been carried out, including the return to its stately livery of the South Eastern & Chatham, dark lake and gold.

It is probable that, at York, *Topaz*, built in 1913 in the heyday of railways, is admired by far more people than ever it was during its years in service, when Pullmans were rather more common. The Birmingham Railway Carriage & Wagon Company alone built them for forty-one years, many being exported.

Private collectors can buy smaller mementoes of the works' output. In 1985, a dealer was offering wagon plates dated between 1913 and 1954 at up to £17.50 each.

Road builders have appropriated far more land in Smethwick than did railways. And north of Handsworth Junction, the trackbed hides in a deep cutting, now landscaped, and slips unobtrusively beneath the dual carriageway of Kenrick Way, feeding traffic in and out of junction 1 of the M5, which lies alongside.

There are few places where transport contrasts are sharper, for if you stop to view or walk the trackbed you generally find a landscape devoid of humans, except those encapsulated in the cars, coaches and lorries rushing ceaselessly by.

Another busy new road and dead trackbed get together $1\frac{1}{4}$ miles away in the centre of West Bromwich, but here the scenario is different. There are people, some walking the trackbed to exercise themselves or their dogs; others, laden with shopping, are walking from a large new centre to buses. The latter choose one of the glass bus shelters lining the town-centre gyratory ringway. They have the choice of a view across to the shopping centre or, alongside, a gently dipping area of grass that was once the town's modest, yet busy, station. Its platforms remain to give an historical flavour to a new landscape.

In case you are not conscious of this, for the platforms blend well with the grass, a noticeboard states that the area is part of the Handsworth Junction to Swan Village section of the 'Low Level Line'. This is surely a hark-back to the days of the living railway, for West Bromwich is not on a Birmingham–Wolverhampton railway route any more, and the Stour Valley is a mile to the west in Oldbury. The board states that the section has been retained by West Midlands County Council with Department of the Environment support.

If you pause to read the board (I assume it is still there), to copy its message or simply enjoy the pleasant open area, you may become conscious of the scent of the grass, unexpected with so much traffic about.

No one who knows the West Midlands, nor any addict of industrial locomotives, will be under the illusion that Swan Village is a remote rural haven among fields. Rather it is the site of notable gas works, which were the largest in Britain when they opened in 1829.

In more recent years, they were served by a variety of 0–4–0 tanks able to negotiate the sharp curves. The locomotives won the affection of enthusiasts as they shunted sidings and became dwarfed under the shadow of the towering gas holders.

Like the main line, the sidings have gone, and now children

London Midland Region

Divisional Press Office. Rail House
Broad Street, Birmingham 1
Telephone : Midland 4444
Extensions 2303/4/5

Ref:PR16/2377
25.2.72

BIRMINGHAM SNOW HILL TO WOLVERHAMPTON LOW LEVEL
WITHDRAWAL OF PASSENGER TRAINS.

After receiving the consent of the Secretary of State for the
Department of the Environment to withdraw the passenger service from
Birmingham Snow Hill to Langley Green and Wolverhampton, British Rail will
be running the last trains on Saturday 4th March. It is anticipated that a
considerable number of passengers will wish to make a "sentimental" last
journey and the number of coaches used on each train will be increased.

Souvenir Tickets allowing a single journey between Birmingham
Snow Hill and Wolverhampton Low Level or intermediately on 4th March are
on sale at Birmingham New Street and Wolverhampton High Level Ticket
Offices at a cost of 29p each from Monday. The ticket may be retained
after the journey has been made. Postal applications should be made to
the Area Manager, British Rail, Wolverhampton.

The times of the trains which call at all stations on Saturday
are :-

From : Birmingham   06.50,   07.32,   08.15,   12.40,   16.25,   17.10,   17.48
      Snow Hill.

From : Wolverhampton   06.50,   07.32,   08.15,   13.50,   16.25,   17.09,   17.47
      Low Level

END

How the London Midland Region prepared for a sentimental journey ...
souvenir tickets, extra coaches ...

play on the manicured trackbed, able to jump off platform
edges in safety since the trackbed has been infilled to only a few
inches below their level.

Gone are the four signal-boxes: Swan Village North, open
continuously on weekdays; Swan Village Junction South,
which opened at 5.30am, followed 15 minutes later by Swan
Village West, and 15 minutes after that by Swan Village
Basin. This box remained open until 'After departure of no. 33

Bank Train', usually in early evening. This locomotive departed from Cannock Road, Wolverhampton, at 4am and made a trip from Swan Village Basin to the Junction to change men. It was 'Not to convey traffic for West Bromwich'.

Special instructions issued to Swan Village signalmen included details of when it was necessary for express passenger trains and meat trains 'to have a clear run from Wednesbury Central to West Bromwich'.

Railway presence remained at Swan Village until the closure in 1982 of a small coal concentration depot, which had been established just north of Swan Lane level-crossing. It was served by trains which reversed at Wednesbury after running over the spur from the South Staffordshire, and ran south through Swan Village tunnel (412yd), at the approach to the depot.

Local stations were plagued by vandals so badly that in 1971 buildings at unstaffed ones were demolished. The intention was to substitute bus-stop shelters if a switch in policy brought about retention of the dmu service. It was something not then considered likely.

From Wednesbury, the singled line continued through Priestfield to sidings about a quarter of a mile north (visible from Wolverhampton Road overbridge), at the approach to Wolverhampton Steel Terminal at Monmore Green, lying above the BW & D, and below the Stour Valley route. But as recession continued, the stretch from Wednesbury to the terminal closed in May 1983, leaving it to be served from the Stour Valley.

Among the expresses about which the Swan Village signalmen were given instructions were the Paddington–Birkenhead services and others from Kent, 'Sunny South' territory which took Southern Green coaches into Birkenhead (Woodside); and the Cornishman, with a pedigree dating back to 1908 when the GWR developed its Birmingham–Bristol route in rivalry with the Midland (see Volume 13 of this series).

In the late 1950s you could book seats at West Bromwich, Wednesbury Central and Bilston Central for 2 shillings (10p) and catch the Cornishman from those stations: there was no need to go to Snow Hill. But the journey was slow, taking 40min between Wolverhampton and Snow Hill and, overall, 2hr longer than today to reach Penzance.

Non-stop runs over the BW & D were made by the short-lived Birmingham Pullman of the 1960s (see Volume 7 of this series). It began and ended two of its four weekday shuttles between Paddington and Snow Hill at Wolverhampton because it was based at Cannock Road.

The rest of the main line, deep in cutting and tunnel to Wolverhampton Low Level, has gone. If you look over the bridge parapet in Lower Walsall Street by the terminal entrance, the twin bores of the station approach tunnels (377yd) stare at you like giant eyes, full of sadness, memory and regret.

How different was the GWR approach to Birmingham from the south, with the generously laid-out four tracks and spacious stations to match. Wolverhampton Low Level never inspired the affection bestowed on Snow Hill and remains dominated by the tall retaining wall of the Stour Valley line and High Level, into which is inserted a draughty colonnade used by pedestrians between High Level station—simply 'Wolverhampton' today—and Wednesfield Road. The colonnade provides a restricted view of Low Level station, which finally ceased active life when it closed as a parcels concentration depot in 1982.

Wolverhampton Low Level–Cannock Road, a short but historically complicated stretch intrinsic to Wolverhampton's railways, is dealt with in Chapter 4.

Closing the Dudley–Wolverhampton stretch of the Oxford Worcester & Wolverhampton pruned the most heavily industrialised section from that mainly rural route. Withdrawal of Snow Hill–Wolverhampton passenger services eradicated virtually the only industrialised stretch of the Paddington–Wolverhampton main line. The Stour Valley route between Birmingham and Wolverhampton is not edifying, but its vistas are wider than were those of the Great Western because it tends to climb above the roof-tops, especially on the

BRITISH RAILWAYS

IMPROVED
SLEEPING CAR
SERVICE

BIRKENHEAD — LONDON
(WOODSIDE) (PADDINGTON)

LEAVING BIRKENHEAD 1 HOUR 40 MINUTES LATER

Commencing 13th June 1955, the FIRST and THIRD CLASS SLEEPING CAR advertised on the 7.15 p.m. Birkenhead (Woodside) to London (Paddington) will leave Birkenhead (Woodside) at 8.55 p.m., arriving London (Paddington) at 5.10 a.m.

PRINCIPAL STATIONS SERVED—					Monday to Saturday Nights
Birkenhead (Woodside)	..	..	..	..	dep. 8.55 p.m.
Chester (General) ..	..	..	..	..	dep. 9.45 p.m.
Wrexham General ..	..	..	..	..	dep. 10. 7 p.m.
Ruabon ..	..	..	..	..	dep. 10.18 p.m.
Gobowen ..	..	..	..	..	dep. 10.32 p.m.
Shrewsbury ..	..	..	..	..	dep. 11.10 p.m.
Wellington ..	..	..	..	..	dep. 11.30 p.m.
Wolverhampton (Low Level) ..	..	..	..	dep. 12.20 a.m.
Birmingham (Snow Hill)	..	..	..	..	{ arr. 12.40 a.m. { dep. 1. 0 a.m.
Paddington ..	..	..	..	..	arr. 5.10 a.m.

On arrival at Paddington, passengers may remain in the sleeping car until 8.0 a.m.
The facility is available to passengers joining or alighting at any intermediate station at which this train calls.

The First and Third Class Sleeping Car will continue to be conveyed on the 12.5 a.m. PADDINGTON to BIRKENHEAD (Woodside) on Monday to Saturday mornings inclusive as already advertised

---

SLEEPING BERTH CHARGES

1st Class, 27s. 0d. per person in addition to the 1st Class Fare
3rd Class, 11s. 0d. per person in addition to the 3rd Class Fare

Application for Berths specifying class, number required and whether for Lady or Gentleman, or for both, should be made to :—

STATION MASTER'S OFFICE, PADDINGTON.
DISTRICT OPERATING SUPERINTENDENT, CHESTER.
or to any Station.

Full details may be obtained from Stations, Offices and Agencies.

Printed in England by Joseph Wones Ltd., West Bromwich ; also at Birmingham and London.

The improved sleeping car service between Birkenhead (Woodside) and Paddington made a brisk, 20 minute run between Wolverhampton and Birmingham, only to wait at Snow Hill for a similar period

Wolverhampton approach, while the GWR picked its way through tunnels and cuttings.

Swan Village–Great Bridge (Horseley Fields Junction)

Like Priestfield, Swan Village station needed four platforms because it was a junction. Its branch ran 1½ miles to the South Staffordshire at Great Bridge. It was authorised in the BW & D Incorporation Act of 1846 and was politically important because the Act included powers for the BW & D to continue the line to Dudley if the SSR did not do so by 1 November 1849, which, by a hair's breadth, it did. The BW & D had running powers through to Dudley while the SSR was given access to Wolverhampton over the BW & D from Wednesbury.

Once the 'race to Dudley' was settled, local railway building slackened and seventeen years elapsed before GWR Birmingham–Dudley passengers had a direct route they could call their own, and were relieved of the burden of travelling via Wolverhampton (Low Level) with all the extra mileage and misery that entailed.

The Birmingham (Snow Hill)–Dudley passenger service survived for ninety-eight years—until 1964. Afterwards the branch was retained as a diversionary route, though only for three years. The last closure was between Swan Village and the canal basin, where a short branch and sidings had also opened in 1866. The branch was also busy because it provided access to the large Swan Village gas works, which still dominate the area.

Duddeston Viaduct

Can a scheme, not even a railway, which only got as far as being crowned with some 200yd of track be classed as a forgotten railway? Some of the most striking and substantial remains in central Birmingham are those of Duddeston viaduct. It followed a ½ mile shallow S-shaped route, either on overbridge or embankment, at roughly twice roof-top height, running, unconnected, from the Birmingham & Oxford at the approach to Moor Street station, to the London & North Western just south of the New Street tunnel. The only track that it ever carried stretched 200yd from the B & O and its only use was as a siding for washing cattle trucks.

The viaduct remains are best seen from the carriage window, for the lines at both ends are either level with, or above, the viaduct remains.

The B & O's original powers of 1846 for a connection to the LNWR near Curzon Street were modified to avoid the LNWR crossing the Oxford spur on the level. When the B & O sought a connection near New Street, Euston feared their rivals for London traffic would be able to use New Street and not have to face the high cost of building a Birmingham station of their own. Also, rivals using New Street might get to Wolverhampton by exercising running powers over the Stour Valley line.

The Commons supported Brunel's application for only 14 chains of land but the Lords disagreed. The Oxford company then resumed work on the originally projected Duddeston link, but only as far as their own boundary.

Then Euston and Paddington settled their differences and neither needed the link. Construction stopped and the only work in over 130 years has been the gradual demolition of the embankment to allow the expansion of industrial buildings. But it seems to have been rather like a mouse nibbling at a giant sausage, and so the vistas remain.

If the embankment remains long enough, an ignorant historian may one day mistake it for a post-Roman wall, rather than recognising it as a remnant of political 'stonewalling' by two companies playing for the high stakes of lucrative traffic between Britain's two largest cities.

Henley-in-Arden Branch

The Great Western liked to call the rolling countryside south of Birmingham its 'Beautiful Borderlands'. Through it ran two branches which were joined to the Birmingham & North Warwickshire once that was built. They were Bearley–Alcester (see Volume 3 of this series) and Lapworth (Rowington Junction)–Henley-in-Arden, the latter a small, delightful, busy town. A company originally got powers for a line of only 3¼ miles in 1861, yet it was 1894 before the sleepy countryside awoke to a branch, constructed by the Birmingham & Henley-in-Arden Railway. Trains ran to a terminus at the north end of the main street until, in 1898, the B & NW route opened, and they continue to its new station, which today remains the most spacious and pleasant of those between Birmingham (Moor Street) and Stratford-upon-Avon.

The branch was little used and became an early casualty of World War I, closing within weeks of the outbreak. The section remained between the B & NW and Henley goods station, which incorporated the original terminus, for almost a half century longer, closing at the end of 1962.

There will be another forgotten line in the next edition if BR are successful in carrying out plans to close the 4 miles of the Birmingham and North Warwickshire route south from Henley to Bearley, including Wootton Wawen. (See: J. M. Tolson, 'One Way for Henley?' *Railway Magazine*, March 1985.)

CHAPTER 3

Birmingham: LNWR

The system that survives and thrives

It is perhaps a good thing that railway companies are no longer in a position to gloat over the misfortunes of their rivals. For what a field day the LNWR would have had as the GWR's system based on Snow Hill was torn to pieces, while its own remained virtually intact and was electrified and improved.

While the GWR lost its Birmingham–Wolverhampton main line, the only former LNWR casualties within the Birmingham city boundary were three short branches. The longest, of only 2½ miles, was the Harborne Railway.

Harborne Railway

'Did you see a fox?' asks an informative leaflet by Birmingham City Parks Department about the Harborne Line Walkway. I never realised that they live so close to the city's heart. Are they descendants of foxes which kept a wily eye on commuter trains that ran for over half a century until 1934, and goods trains that continued for another three decades? From a mass of press cuttings that Birmingham planners sent me, I deduce that the Harborne Railway is better loved in death than ever it was in life. For did not people living in the large terraced houses flanking wide, tree-shaded roads, desert it for trams and buses which ran into the city centre more directly and with greater ease than the branch trains, which had to take their place between expresses on the congested Stour Valley line?

The walkway, from which you may also see peacocks, butterflies, squirrels, greenfinches and house martins, begins as an addition to Summerfield Park, slips into cutting here and there, marked by overbridges, and ends on an embankment by a high bridge over Park Hill Road, just short of where the Harborne terminus yard once ended. The embankment provides splendid views over the wooded suburb.

The branch *might* have been open still had it been built in its proposed form from Soho to the Halesowen–Bromsgrove branch at Lapal. Landowners' objections stifled that scheme, and eventually the 2½ mile branch to Harborne was completed in 1874, 8 years 2 months after authorisation. Once the passenger service fell victim to road competition, coal traffic to Mitchell & Butler's brewery, and depots at Hagley Road and Harborne stations, kept it alive.

The 1934 passenger closure was a sentimental occasion, a reporter writing of ghosts who haunted him as he walked up and down no. 1 platform at New Street before the departure of the last 'Harborne Express'.

> They were bewhiskered, cheery-faced old gentlemen who wore bowler hats and carried bags and told funny stories by the dozen; middle-aged matrons who carried shopping baskets and apparently inexhaustible supplies of gossip; callow youths, so conscious of their first long trousers—all the people, in fact, who over the last 60 years had been travelling by the 'Harborne Express'.

The 'Harborne expresses' were notable for having been worked throughout their life almost exclusively by Webb tanks: 2–4–2 and 0–6–2 the coal tanks. The tanks had a tough time with trains which loaded up to eight coaches in Edwardian days, when passenger traffic was heaviest. In later years, goods, coal and brewery trains were generally worked by

L.N.W.] BIRMINGHAM (New Street) and HARBORNE—Weekdays only.

Platform	1	2	1		1	1		1	3		3	1	1	1	1	1	1	1	2	1	1	1	1	1	1	1	1
	A.M	A.M	A.M		A.M	A.M		NON	P.M		P.M	P.M	P.M	P.M	P.M	P.M	P.M	P.M	P.M	P.M	P.M	P.M	P.M	P.M	P.M	P.M	P.M
Birm. (New St.) ..	7 0	7 45	9 5	....	1010	1110	..	1215	1250	....	1S10	1X15	1S20	1S50	2 15	3 15	4 15	4X50	5 15	5X35	5X58	6X15	6 35	7X 0	7 20		
Monument Lane ..	7 5	7 48	9 8	....	1013	1113	..	1218	1254	....	1S13	1X18	1S24	1S53	2 19	3 18	4 18	4X53	5 18	5X38	..	6X18	6 38	7X 4	7 23		
Icknield Port Rd..	7 6	7 51	9 11	..	1016	1116	...	1221	1257	....	1X21	1S27	1S56	2 22	3 21	4 21	4X56	5 21	5X41	..	6X21	6 41	7X 6	7 25			
Rotton Park Rd. ..	7 9	7 54	9 15	..	1019	1119	..	1224	1 0	..	1X24	1S30	1S59	2 25	3 24	4 24	4X59	5 24	5X44	6X 4	6X24	6 44	7X 9	7 28			
Hagley Road	7 12	7 57	9 1×	....	1022	1122	....	1227	1 5	....	1S19	1X27	1S35	2S 3	2 28	3 27	4 27	5X 2	5 28	5X47	6X 7	6X27	6 47	7X11	7 32		
Harborne	7 16	8 1	9 22	..	1026	1126	..	1231	1 7	..	1S23	1X31	1S37	2S 7	2 32	3 31	4 31	5X 6	5 32	5X51	6X11	6X32	6 52	7X16	7 37		

Platform	1	1	1	1	1	1	2	2			A M	A.M	A.M	A.M	A.M	A.M	A.M	A.M	A.M	A.M	A.M	A.M	A M
	P.M	P.M	P.M	P.M	P.M	P.M	P.M	P.M															
Birm. (New St.) ..	7X40	8 15	8X50	9 20	10 0	1040	1055	1190		Harborne	5 35	6 55	7 25	7 48	8 8	8 24	8 53	8 53	9 10	9 53	10 5	1055
Monument Lane ..	7X44	8 19	...	9 23	10 3	..	1059	1124		Hagley Road	5 37	6 57	7 27	7 50	8 10	8 26	8 55	8 55	9 12	9 55	10 7	1057
Icknield Port Rd..	7X47	8 21	···	9 26	10 6	1045	11 2	1127		Rotton Park Rd. ..	5 40	6 40	7 30	7 54	8 13	8 29	8 59	8 59	9 15	9 58	1010	1040
Rotton Park Rd. ..	7X50	8 24	8X56	9 29	10 9	1048	11 6	1130		Icknield Port Rd..	5 42	6 42	7 32	7 57	8 15	8 31	8 45	9 0	9 17	9 40	1012	1042
Hagley Road	7X54	8 27	8X59	9 32	1012	1051	11 9	1133		Monument Lane ..	5 45	6 45	7 35	8 0	8 19	8 33	....	9 5	9 20	9 45	1016	1045
Harborne	7X57	8 31	9X 3	9 36	1016	1055	1113	1137		Birm. (New St.) ..	5 51	6 51	7 41	8 6	8 25	..	8 50	9 9	9 26	9 50	1021	1051

	A.M	P.M	P.M	P.M	P.M	P.M		P.M	P.M	P.M		P M	P.M		P.M	P.M	P.M	P.M	
Harborne	1140	1242	..	1X50	1S55	2X 8	2 40	...	3 40	4 40	....	5 20	5X58	6 40	...	7X25	7 45	...	8 40	9 45	1025	11 0	....
Hagley Road	1142	1244	..	1X52	1S57	2X10	2 42	..	3 42	4 42	...	5 22	6X 0	6 42	...	7X27	7 47	..	8 42	9 47	1027	11 3	..
Rotton Park Rd. ..	1145	1247	..	1X55	2S 0	2X13	2 45	...	3 45	4 45	...	5 25	6X 4	6 45	...	7X30	7 50	...	8 45	9 50	1030	11 6	...
Icknield Port Rd..	1148	1249	..	1X57	2S 3	2X16	2 47	...	3 47	4 47	...	5 29	6X 6	6 48	...	7X32	7 52	...	8 47	9 52	1032	11 8	...
Monument Lane ..	1151	1252	..	2X 0	2S 6	2X20	2 50	...	3 50	4 50	...	5 32	6X 9	6 51	...	7X35	7 55	...	8 50	9 55	1035	1111	...
Birm. (New St.) ..	1157	1258	..	2X 6	2S12	2X26	2 56	...	3 56	4 56	...	5 37	6X15	6 57	...	7X41	6 1	..	8 56	10 1	1041	1117	...

S Sats. only.   X Sats excepted.

The Harborne branch timetable from the Birmingham Gazette & Express Railway Guide, February, 1907, showing departure platforms of trains from New Street station

ex-Midland class 2F 0–6–0s. These continued to endow the branch with a yesteryear flavour up to total closure in 1963.

They, too, were shapely locomotives, with tall chimneys, large boiler domes, large round spy-glasses and also open footplates—ideal for spotting foxes!

Curzon Street goods station

Locating the goods depots through which the LNWR and Midland Railways handled the raw materials and products of a thousand trades is a comparatively easy job, but the only place where there is a memorial worth seeing is at Birmingham Curzon Street.

Never as famous or as controversial as the Euston Arch, its northern counterpart, the square, pillared mass of Curzon Street original building survives as a memorial to the designer

London and North Western Railway.
TELEPHONE No. 29.

Memo. FROM J. LISLE,
GOODS AND CARTAGE DEPARTMENT,
London and North Western Railway,
WALSALL.   190

GREAT WESTERN RAILWAY.   Department.
(45)
MEMORANDUM from

MIDLAND RAILWAY,   190
From CENTRAL STATION,
BIRMINGHAM.

Goods departments dealt with endless flows of memos . . . An LNWR Goods
and Cartage Department, a GWR Post Department, and the Midland's
Central goods station in Birmingham, sent these in early Edwardian days.
The Clear, spidery pen and ink writing was remarkably similar

of both, Philip Hardwick. The public outrage over the demolition of the Euston Arch probably helped to save Curzon Street when British Rail applied to demolish it even though it was a Grade 1 Listed Building.

It was bought for a nominal sum by Birmingham City Council in 1978 as a prelude to restoration that received a Civic Trust award five years later. When it won the industrial class in the 1984 Royal Institution of Chartered Surveyors conservation awards, the judges described it as 'a monument to Birmingham, the railway age, Victorian self-confidence and the architecture of the day'.

The building owes its air of detachment from neighbouring buildings to the demolition of the hotel which took the place of the ornate flanking arches Hardwick had designed. It is easy to spot, lying just east of the London & Birmingham main line, of which it was the original Birmingham terminal. It was used until the new route was built into New Street Station. The building towers above a large, wide, single-storey shed of what in recent years was Lawley Street parcels concentration depot. For years, Lawley Street was enormously busy with a main goods shed and yard that could absorb 412 wagons; a partially covered grain depot for 165; a coal wharf for 163; a vegetable depot (137); and, smallest of all yet still appreciable in size, a four-siding 'depot' for 60 fish wagons.

Aston: Windsor Street Goods Branch

Almost as close to the city's heart is Aston, a district where the LNWR had tremendous presence. Aston locomotive shed was rebuilt into its final form of twelve roads after the opening, in 1880, of the Aston Windsor Street goods branch. It left the Grand Junction almost opposite the shed and ran west for almost a mile towards the centre of Birmingham. It fed Walter Street goods depot, which could hold almost 250 wagons; the main yard at Aston, 30 more; and Windsor Street goods and coal yard, at branch end, 334. Additionally, the branch provided the access to extensive sidings of Birmingham

WOLVERHAMPTON: *Plate 5 (above)* the original carriage entrance to High Level station is among memorials to the LNWR and its allies. In 1985 it still awaited restoration, looking strangely isolated, attached buildings having been demolished; *Plate 6 (below)* winter sunshine catches Wolverhampton Low Level and its quasi-stately main building, which has a notable and lofty entrance hall. 2 January 1959.

FREIGHT: *Plate 7 (above)* first junction north of Wolverhampton (Low Level) was Cannock Road, abolished when the Oxley Chord Line opened 9 August 1983. Ironbridge Power Station to Silverdale Colliery, Stoke, MGR train reversing with Class 50 No 50041, 7 April 1975; *Plate 8 (below)* Oxley Marshalling Yard about 1923, being shunted by Stafford Road Works built Saddle tanks. The extensive yard, made redundant by electrification, provided the site for a large carriage maintenance depot, to which 25 Kv electrification was extended.

Corporation Gas Works and to others, which were maintained privately.

In its final decade, the branch was the southern terminus of one of a rare species—a BR named freight: Condor, a fitted, overnight service, introduced in 1963, between Aston and Glasgow Gushetfaulds depot. It was a forerunner of Freight-liner trains, which helped to make branches like Windsor Street outdated. Before it closed in 1970, the main terminal was known as Aston Goods and Windsor Street Steel terminal.

Soho Pool Goods

Third and last of the LNWR goods branches within hailing distance of central Birmingham was that to Soho Pool, opened in 1887. It was fed by a single track which stemmed from the Soho–Perry Barr loop, descending past the island platform of Soho Road station (closed as a wartime economy in 1941). After passing Piers Road, a siding to Birmingham Corporation Electricity Works, the branch fanned out into twelve sidings, with a thirteenth serving a small goods shed on the west side.

The yard's capacity was 486 wagons and it was busy for years, surviving until 1974 for general traffic, and as a Texaco fuel oil depot until complete closure in 1982. The approach trackbed is easy to spot from Soho Loop trains, which also cross the Birmingham Snow Hill–Wolverhampton Low Level trackbed close-by.

CHAPTER 4

Wolverhampton

Locomotive birthplace; broad gauge deathbed

Memories live longer than dreams. At least that was what I was trying to make them do as I leaned on the parapet of the wide bridge carrying Wolverhampton Road over the route once taken by the Kings and Castles between that town and Birmingham. My sunny Saturday afternoon reverie was interrupted by a couple who stopped their car and asked directions to a garden centre. Their confident tones suggested they were in no doubt that they were talking to someone who lived locally.

But I had never stood on that bridge before, although I'd passed underneath on expresses whose smoky locomotives had helped to blacken the arches beneath my feet. Perhaps I looked locally knowledgeable because I was totally absorbed in the scene. Only one track still lay on the wide trackbed below, but in my mind's eye, I quickly relaid the missing ones and timetabled trains on them: one facet of the fun and satisfaction to be enjoyed in hunting old railways.

One of the great attractions and joys of Wolverhampton's old railways is that you can still find satisfying clues to their variety, especially by examining engineering works. Their character is born of a legacy of several major companies which became parts of the Great Western, the London & North Western and the Midland.

OW & W: Priestfield Junction–Cannock Road Junction

While the LNWR took its Stour Valley line across the rooftops to get through Wolverhampton, mostly on viaduct or embankment, the broad-gauge invasion of the Oxford Worcester & Wolverhampton went deep.

It drove north from Priestfield, its junction with the Birmingham Wolverhampton & Dudley (Chapter 2) mainly in cuttings, broad and shallow, or narrow and deep. Excavations and tunnelling partly accounted for the passing of nine years between the authorisation of the route and its opening in 1854.

If you are architecturally minded, you may regret that you can no longer walk into the lofty booking hall of Wolverhampton (Low Level) station with 'a fine carved ceiling', to quote Gordon Biddle (*Railway World*, June 1955). But it is the life of a station, rather than its buildings, that is best deserving of memory. Low Level was among the stations where GWR staff supplied 'hot luncheons'. Tea baskets and cups of tea were supplied on the platforms and staff were instructed that 'passengers are allowed to take the cups and saucers into the carriage with them'.

Company instructions also laid down that, 'The Staff must remove cups, saucers &cs from carriages after passengers have finished with them . . .'

That done, refreshed passengers might, perhaps, have continued their journey north to Shrewsbury and beyond on an express which soon left the narrow confines of the station layout, passed under Wednesfield Road and a lattice footbridge a little further north as it headed beneath Cannock Road towards Cannock Road Junction. It was here that the OW & W met a natural death on joining the Shrewsbury & Birmingham, and where the GWR dream of broad gauge to the Mersey came to an abrupt end.

Until summer 1983, merry-go-round coal trains between

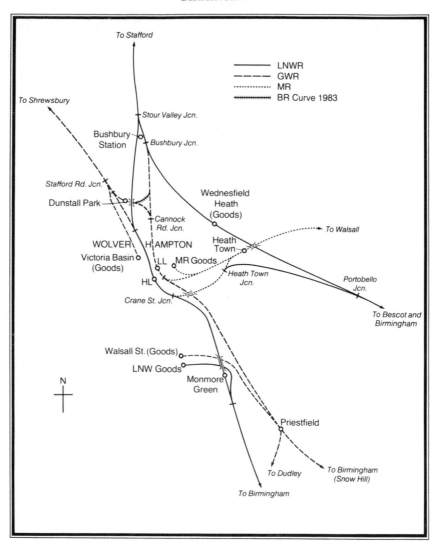

Wolverhampton. The original Shrewsbury & Birmingham spur from Stafford Road Junction to the LNWR was closed for more than a century, from 1859 until restored for electrification in 1966

several pits and the Ironbridge power station 'hiccupped' at Cannock Road, having to reverse along a neck of some 400yd culled from the old main line. But that tedium ended with the opening of a 320yd spur the westerly point of which is just south of a viaduct carrying the Stour Valley line between High Level station and Bushbury. The neighbouring arch once carried two roads from Cannock Road Junction to Stafford Road shed: the route here is easy to define still.

Once the new line – the Oxley Chord – opened, the OW & W tip was lifted and the trackbed offered for sale.

Stafford Road Works

It is difficult to recall the ambience of a works of the size and importance of Stafford Road, amid the cheerfully painted factories that have risen from its ashes. For more than a century (1859–1964), the works built or repaired steam locomotives, but they never rivalled Swindon. Although the GWR acquired Dunstall Hill at Wolverhampton for expansion in 1900, this did not take place until 1932 for 'financial reasons'. Always, Swindon could cope.

The same railway-establishment-to-factory fate befell the LNWR's main locomotive shed at Bushbury, only a short distance away, and, in a sense, the remoter Oxley shed of the GWR. The latter's site provided the space needed for an Inter-City carriage maintenance shed in the electrified servicing yard. Besides being rather inaccessible compared with the other sheds, Oxley was never quite as interesting. Although its allocation was well over 100 locomotives in steam days, Stafford Road, with an allocation around 70, was the glamour depot, where the 'big namers' were to be spotted as they were rested and revived.

Wolverhampton: Victoria Basin

Another economy close to the heart of the town was that of the Victoria Basin branch, built by the Shrewsbury & Birmingham when it was at loggerheads with the Stour Valley authorities and had to tranship goods to the canal before establishing its own route to Birmingham over the BW & D. The tranship depot was served by a branch which ran through part of Stafford Road works. The single line closed in 1972, but the large, distinctively GWR, goods shed of Herbert Street goods station, which the company built in 1935, remains, in use as a builders' merchant's premises and easily spotted from the main lines north of Wolverhampton – formerly High Level – station.

More venerable, though less functional, is the two-storey carriage entrance to Queen Street station, as High Level was first known. The building, now detached from surrounding property, stands on the corner of Horseley Fields and is close enough to the station to be seen from the Inter-City carriage window. It still awaits restoration.

The Kingswinford Branch

During its comparatively short life (for it only opened in 1925), the Kingswinford branch was a useful diversionary route carrying through freight and the occasional excursion and summer-holiday empty coaching stock train clear of the congested lines through Wolverhampton (Low Level), and the limited facilities available at Cannock Road carriage sidings. Closure, forty years later, transformed it into a diversionary 'route' of another kind, where people could forget about the cares of town and industrial life, and relax amid nature.

A plethora of direction signs on roads point to pedestrian entrances to the 'Kingswinford Branch Railway Walk', and its car parks, picnic sites and conveniences. The trackbed leads visitors through pleasant, leafy suburbia and a quietly beautiful countryside which they may be surprised to find could lie so close to the heart of Wolverhampton and parts of the Black Country.

The walk takes pressure off local parks, open spaces and beauty spots by opening up an abundance of fresh countryside of charm and visual interest, especially to the enthusiast: cuttings, embankments, bridges.

The Kingswinford branch was a 12¼ mile line about which, although its course did not pass through particularly difficult terrain, the GWR had second thoughts for two decades. It has now been closed for half the length of time that it was open.

After authorisation in 1905, construction was sluggish enough to span the years before and after Grouping. The trackbed has been adapted by two local authorities, Wolverhampton and South Staffordshire, for leisure purposes. Designated Valley Park, the Wolverhampton section, together with James Brindley's Staffordshire & Worcestershire Canal, follows the course of Smestow Brook in a broad valley. Further south, the South Staffordshire District Council christened its 5½ miles the Kingswinford Branch Railway Walk. The branch was actually the southern section of the line, between Baggeridge Junction, with the Pensnett Railway, and the OW & W at Brettell Lane.

Local people generally called it the Wombourn line, a fact perpetuated in the paperback history, *By Rail to Wombourn*, by J. Ned Williams and students of Wulfrun College of Further Education, Wolverhampton.

Wombourn down station building has been adapted as an information centre, while in the station yard, a few feet below, Wombourn Dog Training Club has its headquarters in a large wooden hut. But there is plenty of car parking, and this is a good place to start exploring the route. A council leaflet broadens the scope for visitors, detailing nearby places they might like to know about.

CHAPTER 5

Black Country: GWR

Wolverhampton (Priestfield Junction)–Dudley

Following the July 1962 withdrawal of passenger services over the Oxford Worcester & Wolverhampton between Wolverhampton (Low Level) and Stourbridge Junction, the Western modified its passenger table 164: Birmingham, Worcester and Hereford, Shrewsbury, Hereford and Newport by replacing the local service details for Wolverhampton–Stourbridge Junction with a panel:

RAIL SERVICE WITHDRAWN

Road services are operated in the area by the Birmingham and Midland Motor Omnibus Co. Ltd.

It gave an almost funereal appearance to parts of the table: only a black-edged border seemed to be missing.

The now forgotten element of the route is the 6 miles between Priestfield Junction and Dudley. It had five intermediate stations, while on the still open freight line between Dudley and Stourbridge Junction there were another four. The impact made by the passenger economy on the economic and social life of the area was negligible compared with what was to come in 1980: the closure of Bilston steelworks. They lay across

Coseley Road from Bilston West station. In spring 1982, while young children played on a rope swinging from a tall tree growing on the trackbed, I surveyed the enormous open space that was until recently a skyline-dominating steelworks.

In the distance, works diesels shunted about on demolition duties. They were easy to spot because, apart from being painted bright yellow, the air was clear, no longer polluted by the output of tall chimneys. The half-demolished tall blue sheds were no longer curtained by a screen of smoke thrown up by vintage steam shunters. The sheds stood out against a blue sky, stark as the economic situation which had brought closure to the works.

I was standing on another area of wasteland, a grassy expanse that awaits those who attain the embankment, originally created by the Oxford Worcester & Wolverhampton navvies. It can be reached either by a scramble up its steep flank from Coseley Road, or simply by walking through what was once the station entrance in Coseley Road. The rubble of the platforms lies beneath two low, shapely moulds, which might in the distant future be thought of as twentieth-century tumuli. The rest of the grassy area is the grave of up and down sidings, which once flanked the little station, and small braces of inward and outward steelworks sidings. The Western Region Sectional Appendix for the Birmingham Traffic District in 1960 referred to two of the outward sidings as 'the Banbury Line', and another as Jubilee Siding.

Connected to the GWR sidings at the Wolverhampton end were the steelwork's own Millfields sidings. The end of passenger services, ahead of the Beeching Report, was followed in 1968 by complete closure between Priestfield Junction and Dudley North Junction, the steelworks continuing to be served from the Stour Valley line.

A search for the remains of this, the northern end of the OW & W, makes it easy to discover why local people preferred buses, cars, coaches, motor bikes and cycles. The railway's route was not convenient. To find a cutting through which trains ran to reach Bilston West from Wolverhampton and

Priestfield means leaving main and busy roads and twisting through a housing estate, established well into the railway age, and yet never served by it.

The cutting is now a walkway, created by municipal planners anxious to improve local image and amenity. They have done it well. Dropping into the cutting, one gets away from the monotonous views of houses, streets and works. Yet the transition to an area a little more suggestive of the country is not quite satisfying for you feel you are walking in a trench. But you soon have to climb out again for a bridge carrying Millfields Road has been replaced by an embankment, by the infilling of the railway cutting. Beyond Bilston West, the trackbed continues on a low, curving embankment, reclaimed and landscaped, towards Daisy Bank, where the trackbed becomes a vaguely identifiable component of a landscaping scheme.

Princes End station site can be identified by a narrow, grassy slope which climbed from platform level to Fountain Lane. After parking (carefully since this deceptively narrow road is far busier than its width suggests), it is worth peering over the bridge. Ignore the rubbish-strewn cutting, where the station once lay, and look west towards Dudley, for tracks are visible. They stable wagons awaiting repair at the South Staffordshire Wagon Company's works. The sidings end near a lattice footbridge across the OW & W trackbed, which local people used to reach Bloomfield Road. Walking the adjacent footpath, you can get a closer view of the old route, stretching to where the OW & W crossed above the Stour Valley line on an overbridge demolished during electrification, and of the short-lived Bloomfield curve (passengers 1853–61), which allowed through running from Wolverhampton (High Level) to Worcester.

There is a better vantage point on Tipton's new industrial estate, close to where Bloomfield Road dips under the Stour Valley line. An embankment, which carried the OW & W between the Stour Valley bridge and another over the Birmingham Canal just west, was levelled to clear land for the estate and factories now mask the trackbed's route. Levelled earth beside the Stour Valley line covers what was once the curve. The abutments of the OW & W canal and LNWR bridges are useful visual guides in attempts to reconstruct the Bloomfield scene of years ago—bustling with through and local traffic, especially as the GWR served Tipton Basin; the LNWR, the Bloomfield Basin.

As Peter Robinson recalled in his notes for the RCTS (Railway Correspondence and Travel Society) Reunion Railtour of 22 November 1980:

> Rail/canal interchanges were a feature of the Black Country transport network for many years as the older established canals were better able to serve the many factories along their banks; in fact much local traffic travelled by canal until displaced by road competition, rather than by rail.

Bloomfield was earlier noted by Arthur Stokes in his wonderfully evocative short book, *Fifty Years on the Railway*, which he published himself in 1936 to help build a new Methodist church in Solihull. He recalled his first job as a signalman, at Bloomfield crossing, near Tipton, beside a huge clay pit, where blue bricks were made. Because salt was used in their manufacture, the neighbouring area was pervaded by fumes and smoke which turned the signal-box brasses all the colours of a rainbow.

Closure of Bilston steelworks led to the end of the Princes End branch of the LNWR (page 68), leaving Bloomfield Road with disused branches on both sides. Bloomfield Road is part of the main route between Tipton and Dudley. It crosses the Birmingham–Wolverhampton dual carriageway (the A4023) a short distance south of the OW & W, which crossed it on a high bridge. From here, west to the Dudley Freightliner terminal under the wooded slopes of the castle, the trackbed is incorporated into a shuntback. The terminal was virtually closed and mothballed in 1981 when traffic was switched to Lawley Street, Birmingham, because of a large drop in volume as a result of the recession. The FLT occupies what was the

OW & W's Castle goods yard, and part of Dudley passenger station. The LNWR goods yard lay opposite, just east of the passenger station, which was GWR/LNWR Joint.

If you look over the retaining wall of the long, straight and wide Tipton Road, you will see a partial wilderness where the yard once lay. And you will see an empty trackbed under the road, alongside that of the South Staffordshire line heading east. The trackbed used to carry the approach to Dudley Town goods yard. It is now a scrapyard.

Unlike Dudley, Stourbridge is still comparatively well served by passenger services. Birmingham trains now run to New Street, rather than Snow Hill, though a service to both stations may be restored. Stourbridge Junction is an intermediate stop for trains between Birmingham, Kidderminster and Worcester, and it is still possible to spend 2½min shuttling on a single car over the 57 chains between Stourbridge Junction and Town station: BR's much publicised shortest passenger branch. It achieved the status in 1977 when it was shortened by just 2 chains at Stourbridge Town, where a pleasant, ornate station building, befitting a town of Stourbridge's character and importance, was demolished to make way for an extended bus station. The platform with a bus-stop shelter for diesel-'dodger' passengers, now forms stand L.

The cast-iron Vauxhall Road footbridge, which generations of commuters climbed to get to and from the station, became redundant and the only chore for passengers now is a short walk on the level round the buffers. Parliamentary powers were needed for footbridge demolition because it was a public right of way.

The branch had a noteworthy place in GWR history, as noted by the Birmingham Divisional Superintendent A. V. R. Brown in a Debating Society paper in 1948:

> The only self-contained passenger branch in the Birmingham division is that from Stourbridge Junction to Stourbridge Town, ¾ mile in length, worked by an autocar under 'One Engine in Steam' regulations; a parallel line giving connection with the Stourbridge Town Goods Depot.

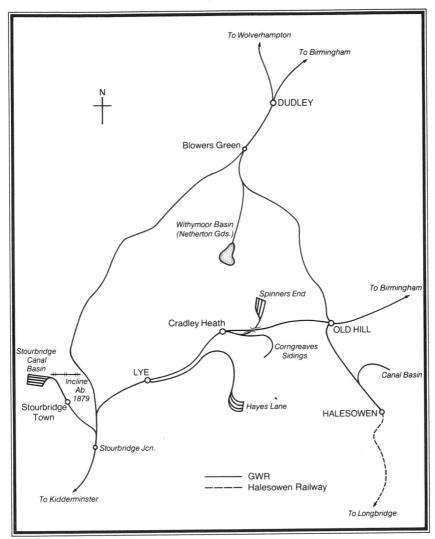

The GWR had several comparatively small but tremendously busy goods branches in the Black Country. All shown here have long gone, but Oldbury survives

GWR Goods Branches

Western Region Working Time Tables distinguished operation of the branch by two titles—Stourbridge Town Passenger Branch, and Stourbridge Basin Goods Branch—until
closure in 1965. Its single line continued north past Town
station and plunged at 1 in 27 down the twisting flank of a hillside to the canal about half a mile beyond the station. It was an
operator's nightmare. Instructions occupied two large pages
in the Sectional Appendix.

'THE STATION MASTER AT STOURBRIDGE TOWN STATION' (the
print emphasised that it was to be him and him alone) had to
check daily that there was a 'good supply' of sprags kept on the
incline ready for use. It was a task which in GWR days was
entrusted to the 'Foreman in the Goods Yard'. Occasionally
there were runaways. The Appendix acknowledged such poss-
ibilities: 'Should an accident occur of such a nature as to
obstruct the adjacent Passenger Single Line all concerned
must take the quickest possible steps to protect the Line...'
Another stipulation was: 'GUARDS MUST RIDE OUTSIDE THEIR
VAN COMPARTMENT AT THE AND BRAKE IN READINESS TO GIVE
INSTANT ATTENTION.'

Railways often improved the quality of life, yet Stourbridge
must have been a noisy place at times. Drivers of tank engines
(tender locomotives were not allowed) were given clear roads
for the climb. They got it by whistling the signalman at Stourbridge Town signal-box at the summit. Three whistles warned
him that a train was ready to run through to the Junction. If it
was stopping at Town station, the local peace was further
disturbed by a crow of the whistle.

Now, only the rumble of diesel engines, bus predominating
over train, disturbs the local atmosphere. An abutment beside
a dual carriageway at the north side of the bus station, and
abutments across the narrow river Stour half-way down the
valley beyond, are still-visible clues to a line once so full of interest.

Such branches had little attraction for spotters, who could

always 'cop' their engines when they were resting in local sheds on Sundays. But they did add character to the old Great Western system in the hilly districts of the Black Country. A passenger between Birmingham (Snow Hill) and Stourbridge over the old GWR route, might see Panniers, or more ancient tanks, at work on several branches, which spun a web around Old Hill.

At nationalisation, the GWR had forty-five yards or groups of sidings in the Black Country triangle—its own term—of Wolverhampton–Stourbridge–Birmingham. Among the yards was Old Hill goods, or Spinners End, as it was known locally. It was unusual in not being directly connected to the nearest main line. Trains reached it over the Corngreaves branch. This left the down (Stourbridge) track at Cradley station and ran 352yd to Cradley End ground frame, which marked the start of Old Hill goods. It continued for about another $\frac{3}{4}$ mile parallel to the Stourbridge line above it, before passing under to reach a goods station, which was actually situated in Cradley Heath, rather than Old Hill.

Gradients, here again, were stiff—stretches of 1 in 40 and 1 in 62 at the worst points—and there were other operating complications, for the station yard was connected to several private factory sidings. At that for Test House, the need was to make sure that wagons did not foul substantial chain-lifting apparatus, and Commercial Department staff had to carry out special instructions after sunset or when it was foggy or snow was falling. Their duty then was to put a white light on the engine stop board about 20yd from the lifting apparatus. To the right of Test House siding was the siding 'which serves the Stone Cracker'. Special instructions applied to that, too.

The Old Hill Goods branch (1907–64) was much younger than its Corngreaves parent, for that dated from 1863, having been authorised with the initial stretch of the Stourbridge Railway from the OW & W at Stourbridge Junction to Old Hill. It produced substantial traffic from the New British Iron Company and brick, clay and engineering works. Another local

G. W. R.	G. W. R.
Rowley Regis and Blackheath	**BILSTON**

4237 G.W.R. TO **CRADLEY HEATH & CRADLEY** 3,000—Est. 337—7/47—(9)—S.	G.W.R. **Princes' End**

G. W. R. **LYE**	G.W.R. **Tipton**

Destination labels, as nostalgic to some enthusiasts as airline tickets

SMALL STATIONS: *Plate 9 (above)* Kingswinford branch. Crewe–Stoke Gifford goods behind No 4901 *Adderley Hall* passes Tettenhall Station, June 1957. Waiting room restored by Wolverhampton Borough Council 1984; *Plate 10 (below)* Swan Village station in its final years. A single unit on the 1710 Birmingham Snow Hill–Wolverhampton Low Level was sufficient even for rush hour service in March 1971. The busy level crossing was controlled from the signal box.

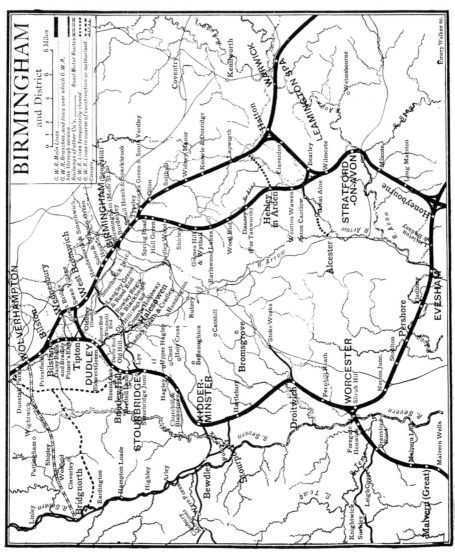

GWR BIRMINGHAM DISTRICT: *Plate 11* map showing 'Road Motor Route' between Wolverhampton and Bridgnorth; the projected Kingswinford branch and that to Bridgnorth, never built. The Henley-in-Arden–Lapworth branch is shown as 'temporarily closed'. Passenger services ceased in 1915.

freight line of 1863 was the Hayes Lane goods line, connected to the goods yard at Lye, where the wooden train staff, round and red, was kept in the signal-box. Also there was the key to a gate near the weighbridge, which had to be kept locked unless the branch was being worked.

Yards and sidings were fed and cleared by a system of 'targeted' Bank Trains, which worked to traffic concentration points. Lye, Hayes Lane and Timmis' Siding Service was served by No. 13 diagram from Stourbridge 'Engine House': Amblecote shed. Six days a week, the locomotive left at 5.55am. Did any spotter ever see it go? If he did, he'd be well into his thirties now for it all ended in 1964.

Time-spans in railway history are constantly lengthening. It's nearly seventy years, for example, since Langley Green became a half-closed station. For its sharply curved platform on the branch to Oldbury has not been used regularly since 30 weekday passenger trains each way were withdrawn in 1915. They were the victims of geography and competition. The branch had opened in 1884 after eleven years in gestation. By then the town's population was 18,000 and growing rapidly. The GWR began a passenger service to Birmingham (Snow Hill) in 1895, to rival the LNWR's to Oldbury & Bromford Lane, on the Stour valley route, about half a mile away on the opposite side of the town centre.

Each route was just over 5 miles and the stopping trains took just over 20min. But while the LNWR trains were through, GWR passengers often had to change to a steam rail-motor at Langley Green, though only for the 3min journey to the branch terminus.

The LNWR kept its hold on Oldbury traffic by offering luggage deliveries from its station, where it handled horses and carriages. No such facilities were available from the GWR, although by 1910 its station staff were handling telephone inquiries.

Oldbury goods depot remained busy until 1964 when the branch was cut back to its present terminus in the Albright & Wilson chemical works, close to the M5 motorway. The branch is now truncated to ½ mile, a third of its original length, though it remains in constant use. In 1980 the government contributed half of the quarter of a million pounds spent by the company replacing sidings so as to keep chemical traffic, including chlorine and caustic soda, off the roads.

Because of the short and congested nature of the branch, sidings were provided at Oldbury & Langley Green, as the station was called in the 1960s.

Lines to Halesowen

Not only can the railway enthusiast no longer find a railway in Halesowen, he cannot always find a bed. An inn at which I called for accommodation during my quest for the town's forgotten lines did not take guests at weekends, and I was directed to Stourbridge. There I found the Talbot Hotel, from where, I remembered, a century and more ago, the Birmingham & Gloucester Railway issued three-part tickets to long-distance travellers. The first portion was for a stage coach to Birmingham, then the nearest railhead; the second for a train from there; and the third portion was the accountant's counterfoil. Stourbridge library has a well preserved example that is worth inspection.

After an overnight stay at the Talbot, I drove over the green and rolling Clent Hills, which come as a rewarding surprise to visitors from afar who think of Birmingham and the Black Country as nothing more than an industrial mass. In glorious, if lukewarm, spring sunshine, I resumed my search for the lost railways of Halesowen, a loose term applying to three lines.

The three lines are remembered for their variety of locomotion, for before pannier tanks became dominant, there were a variety of small GWR tanks, steam railmotors and, towards closure, GWR streamlined railcars. The Halesowen Railway was the haunt of long-surviving Midland engines including outside-frame Kirtley 0–6–0s.

I know of no geography examination paper which includes questions on the railways of Halesowen. Certainly, an examiner preparing such questions would need to allow himself extra time to compose them—and his pupils extra time to answer them! Such are the transport complications of the area that the lines can be considered as a group of three. The first is Dudley (Blowers Green Junction)–Old Hill, 2½ miles, for which the West Midland Railway got authority in 1862. This was at the same time as the natural extension from Old Hill to Halesowen, 1½ miles. The Halesowen Railway, Great Western & Midland Joint, was authorised for 6 miles south to the Midland West of England main line at Longbridge, and completed in 1883, only five years after the others as it happened, for construction of all three was slow. The establishment of the Austin motor works at Longbridge provided the branch with traffic for years. A stub survives, curving sharply away from the main line and disappearing into a cutting.

Dudley–Old Hill

As the last passenger trains prepared to shuttle between Dudley and Old Hill under June skies in 1964, the *Express & Star*, Wolverhampton, prepared an obituary of the branch passenger service.

> Not many will mourn its passing, except maybe for pangs of nostalgia. It has had its day. But in the past there is no doubt that it provided a great service to the community.

The paper quoted Guard Bishop of the 6.30pm from Dudley.

> If we get one passenger on this particular train, that's as many as we'll ever get. We may get him twice a week and he usually gets off at Windmill End.

Twenty years later, it seems reasonable to believe that more enthusiasts seek the line's history and remember its past than ever travelled on its trains in the final years. I was once minded to, but never did so, and that made the job of tracing its route the sadder for I had no memory to build on, only regret to assuage as best I could.

From Dudley, the Old Hill auto-trains ran 68 chains to Blowers Green station, 949yd of the route being occupied by Dudley tunnel. Notes for the railtours that still occasionally follow the OW & W pinpoint the Blowers Green platform site deep in a cutting within sight of the tunnel's southern mouth. The platforms were last used in summer 1962 when the station was known as Dudley South & Netherton.

The station opened with the Old Hill branch in 1878, replacing one called Netherton, which had opened when the OW & W extended its passenger service north from Stourbridge to Dudley in December 1852. A small replacement booking hall opened at street, rather than platform level, in the 1930s, and survives. It is in private use.

Across the road—New Road, in fact—the site can be easily traced of Blowers Green Junction, where the Old Hill branch curved sharply south. The trackbed is now incorporated into an industrial area with a humpback overbridge fenced off. Further along New Road, a similar bridge provides a grandstand from which to follow the trackbed approaching from the junction and heading towards the site of Baptist End Halt, a mile from the junction. It lay in a shallow cutting, handy for people living in terraced houses on a steep hillside between the halt and the main road through the village—the Dudley–Halesowen (A459).

Where the branch bridged Baptist End road, there are now tapered, green embankment slopes. Just south lay Windmill End Junction with the Netherton Goods branch, which dropped away at 1 in 51 at the start of its course of almost a mile. It was the destination of many trains whose drivers heeded 10mph restrictions at either Blowers Green or Old Hill Junctions. It was called the Withymoor Canal Basin branch until 1921, but locally the yard's name never changed.

Like the Halesowen Basin branch, it was for many years a busy rail and canal transhipment yard. It was awkward to work for its layout was restricted. It was approached by the branch as it crossed Northfield Road, the Western Region Sectional Appendix decreeing: 'The Rails over the Public Road must be kept clean.' The traffic that was shunted in and out, generally by Pannier tanks, reflected the diverse nature of local industry. For years, the RCH Station Hand Book noted that the yard handled traffic of Baldwin Ltd's blast furnace and slag siding; and Miles Druce & Co's iron depot, where Tarmac Ltd had a siding.

The site of Windmill End Junction is part of a grassy walk-way, and children are now welcome to use a trackbed where their predecessors would have been trespassers. A good van-tage point is the overbridge in St Peter's Road.

As the branch continued south towards Old Hill, it crossed the Dudley Canal within sight of the southern mouth of Netherton tunnel. Windmill End was the only intermediate station, a status which it retained until 1952, when it, too, became a halt. Once, though, it was busy—and not only with passengers.

Michael Hale and Ned Williams noted in their comprehen-sive book *By Rail to Halesowen* (Michael Hale and the Uralia Press, 1974) that: 'Local lads were often to be found sitting round the waiting room fire; the station seems to have been a popular social centre in the thirties!'

Less than ⅓ mile further south lay Darby End Halt, among those which the GWR opened in August 1905. About ½ mile further south, Old Hill was served by High Street Halt, which the town's shoppers found far more convenient than Old Hill station on the Stourbridge line, which the motor trains reached after crossing Beauty Bank and Station Road on a single-span bridge, of which the abutments remain. The Dudley trains ran into the station under a wooden planked footbridge. It is now open to the winds, but it helps the little station to retain some of its character. Much was lost when the wooden station buildings were replaced by bus-stop shelters in 1968.

The railways of Old Hill never quite developed as once hoped, otherwise the enthusiast of today would also have had to search for the route of a direct connection between the Old Hill and Halesowen branches, and a spur from the Dudley branch facing towards Stourbridge. Neither was built and trains from Dudley and Old Hill arrived at Old Hill, facing towards Birmingham; Halesowen trains used a curved platform on the south side of Old Hill station, just short of the junction with the Stourbridge line.

Old Hill–Halesowen

'The nearest passenger station to Halesowen is the Western Region station at Old Hill, just outside the borough and in the neighbouring borough of Rowley Regis. The station is on the main line, 110 miles from Paddington.' The 1955 edition of the Halesowen official guide went on to state, 'The borough is well served by frequent Midland "Red" bus Services.' It listed fifteen routes, including Halesowen–Old Hill–Dudley–Bilston, no. 226. This was much used once the Halesowen–Old Hill auto services were withdrawn, three weeks before Christmas 1927. The closure, however, was not total, because workmen's trains to Longbridge continued to call at Halesowen. They ran until 1958.

The route, from which track was lifted about fifteen years ago after complete closure of the branch in 1969, is easy to trace, for it lies close and parallel to the main road between the towns, on which bus competition was so devastating. The trackbed clings to the eastern flank of the Stour valley. A substantial and unmistakable abutment lies close to the junction of Coombes Road, leading over the hill to Blackheath. The only intermediate stop—Coombes Holloway Halt, opened in 1905—lay just south of the overbridge. It was here that railmotors stopped, and it is here that the embankment has been overlaid by a large car park built level with the supermarket it serves.

The last section to close was between Old Hill and Halesowen Canal basin, reached by a $\frac{3}{4}$ mile branch which climbed at 1 in 38. Even as late as the 1950s, it was busy enough to be allocated three shunting tanks from 5.35am on weekdays. They also banked trains through to Old Hill. For years, drivers using the single branch carried a red, round wooden staff, kept in Halesowen station signal-box.

Halesowen Railway

Enthusiasts of today may find it a little difficult to appreciate how two branches that met head-on to form a through route could be so different in character. There were several reasons why this was so with the Old Hill–Halesowen branch and the Halesowen Railway. The former was purely Great Western, and its route was through an industrial and suburban area. The Halesowen Railway ran through rolling, but mainly empty, countryside, and was a joint line of the GWR and Midland, with Midland influence, through its motive power, being rather the stronger.

Halesowen's two-platform station was of the sort built in prosperous Victorian market towns lying away from main lines. It included a run-round loop between the platforms. After closure in 1964 the site was soon redeveloped and became the Forge industrial estate. It lies on the north side of the Halesowen bypass on the A456 Birmingham–Kidderminster road, the trackbed immediately south having been bisected when the dual carriageway bypass was constructed.

From there, OS maps plot a thin, dotted, slightly twisting route through fields lying close to the A459 Bromsgrove road. Driving south, you come first to Hunnington, where the Blue Bird toffee factory lies in a spacious rural setting. On the opposite side of the main road is the old station, where the main building is a house which, together with the old station approach drive, is private. The building retains its Midland ambience. The drive and station were used by toffee workers who caught the workmen's trains to Longbridge: they never used the public service because that was withdrawn in 1919— six years before the toffee factory was built.

The workmen's trains were a breed on their own: four-wheel coaches, later replaced by clerestory compartment bogies. At their head—and tail sometimes—old, open-cab 0–6–0s, much photographed crossing Dowery Dell tressel viaduct, ½ mile south of Hunnington. The slightly curved structure carried the single track 100ft above stream and fields. It has long gone. Its photographs are more evocative of the past than, I suspect, a site pilgrimage (if this is possible). The appeal of tressel via-ducts arose from their rarity. Dowery Dell was handy for en-thusiasts living in the West Midlands, like the Lickey Incline, with which it shared the same OS 1in map.

On new OS maps, the trackbed is shown continuing south towards the M5 motorway. I met it again in a lane. Beside an unmade farm track, which the branch once crossed, I stopped and chatted to a farmer happy that warmth was returning to the earth after one of the coldest winters he'd known. The back-cloth to the site of our conversation was the trackbed, about to disappear into Round Saw Croft, a woodland where tall trees take over the guardianship of the route, which passed into a deep cutting just north of where it is now pierced by the motorway, at the western end of a virtually straight mile from Frankley services area.

Regaining the trackbed involves crossing the motorway on the gentle hump of Yew Tree Lane overbridge and turning down Frankley Hill Road to a new housing estate. The trackbed is to be found, well below motorway level, in a deep, in-filled cutting within sound, though not sight, of the traffic. From there it follows a straight, downhill course, with fields on the north (Birmingham) side and the new, corporation, estate opposite. It gives the impression of a shallow moat, but in re-ality it has been adapted as a walkway for people living in the cosy-looking houses to reach Holly Hill shopping centre (also new) in safety. But the hard-surfaced walkway offers no shelter from rain, which is perhaps why the centre car park is so well used. Even 'adapted' railways have their limitations.

Several three-arch overbridges have been incorporated into the walkway as features, supplemented by subways under new roads to maintain segregation of pedestrian and motorist. But through no fault of the planners, graffiti experts and rubbish-dumpers have turned trackbed sections into an untidy fringe to the pleasant estate. That, at least, was how I found it.

Close to the BL Longbridge works, the branch is a reality once more, a short section—stemming from the Birmingham–Bristol main line at Longbridge Junction—serving the works. This section lies 'in the wings', as far as the planners are concerned, in case an extension of the Longbridge–Four Oaks Cross-City Line becomes worth while. When the line opened in 1978, the West Midlands Passenger Transport Executive stated that a 'spur' to Frankley from Longbridge could be developed for passengers. The nearest Frankley residents can get by rail at present is Longbridge station, a modern structure which lies close to the site of the LMS main-line station, closed in 1960.

CHAPTER 6

Black Country: LNWR

Dudley: quick rise; quicker decline

Dudley's quite extensive and complicated railway system was developed in a period of about five years from the arrival of the South Staffordshire Railway in 1850 to completion of the OW & W to Wolverhampton in 1854, including the link to Dudley Port (High Level).

A picture of the town in 1871 in the London & North Western official guide said it had a population of 43,782.

> It is seated in the midst of a fine tract of country, somewhat disfigured by the mining operations carried on in the neighbourhood. The district is rich in coal and iron-stone; and the view from the passing train, after the shades of evening have closed o'er the scene, strikingly reminds the traveller of Homer's description of Vulcan's smithy.

The night skies of Dudley were no longer afire by the time the last regular passenger trains ran in and out of the hub of the Black Country over five routes. All went within a period of only two years, before and after the Beeching Report. It noted only Dudley–Walsall for withdrawal. The first economy was Wolverhampton (Low Level)–Dudley–Stourbridge (page 44)—the 'West Midland Line' as the GWR service timetable called it. Those trains ceased to run from 30 July 1962. Two summers later (15 June 1964), Dudley's 9 mile link with Birmingham (Snow Hill) via Great Bridge and Swan Village was severed. Their route was ex South Staffordshire between Dudley and Horseley Fields Junction. Dudley–Old Hill motor trains ended the same day (page 57). Finally, on 6 July 1964, the Dudley to Dudley Port (High Level) and Dudley Port (Low Level) services ended.

Nowadays, enthusiast specials, ever diminishing in frequency as the years lengthen since passenger closures, approach from the west through Dudley tunnel and run into a deep cutting that leads to the site of the joint station. It was developed with island platforms by the SSR in 1850, while the OW & W added a more substantial one, four track-widths to the north, two years later. All was demolished in 1967, leaving a much simplified track layout, including the now mothballed Freightliner terminal, arranged in a shallow 'moat' between Castle Hill and the high retaining wall of Tipton Road.

The special trains curve under the road and head towards Walsall, reaching, six chains short of a mile, the site of Sedgeley Junction, from which a spur climbed to Dudley Port (High Level).

Dudley–Dudley Port (High Level)

The ½ mile double-track route climbed on a shallow S course to the Stour Valley main line just north of the High Level station. It once carried one of Britain's most intensive local services. Euston decreed that Dudley and Dudley Port should have about 70 4min journeys in each direction between 6.08am and just after midnight on weekdays; less than 20 on Sundays – although still a substantial service for the Sabbath.

Intermingled were a handful of through trains from Birmingham, both express and stopping all stations, and also a luncheon-car express from Dudley to Euston.

The course of much of the spur, up which two-coach trains were pulled by Webb's tall-chimneyed 2–4–2 tanks, could be followed from the carriage window of Stour Valley trains for many years. But now it has disappeared without trace, its earthworks bulldozed to the lower level of the South Stafford-shire line, and its site occupied by a private housing estate built in 1983.

No longer do the smuts or aroma of the hard-pounding tanks swirl across local gardens, or over the roofs of carriages stabled in sidings on the south side of the spur.

Dudley Port (Low Level) was reached from Dudley in five minutes by trains bound for Walsall or beyond. The Dudley Port stations were connected by footpath and sometimes passengers were directed from one to the other to catch the next convenient connection.

Again, the LNWR official guide:

> Leaving Dudley, we pass through Dudley Port Junction by the low level line, and reach Great Bridge and Wednesbury, the latter a junction station for Darlaston and Tipton, and a place of considerable importance in the iron trade.

Centred on iron and coal mines, Wednesbury expanded at a tremendous pace, producing a host of iron products ranging from railway carriages to gun springs. Two important local lines—the Darlaston Loop and the Princes End branch, of almost identical length—were authorised in summer 1855.

Four years later, powers were obtained for an extension of time for completion. That eventually took place in 1863, Wednesbury getting a new station when the branches opened on 14 September. In 1869, Wednesbury became a parliamentary borough, incorporating the parishes of Darlaston and Tipton.

Darlaston Loop

It was in their character that the lines were different. The Princes End branch was the more important as it joined two of the LNWR main lines in the Black Country, although it was built to serve ever growing industry. It was doubled in 1872. To research the Loop is to discover a microcosm of industry which had its roots in the Industrial Revolution. From the

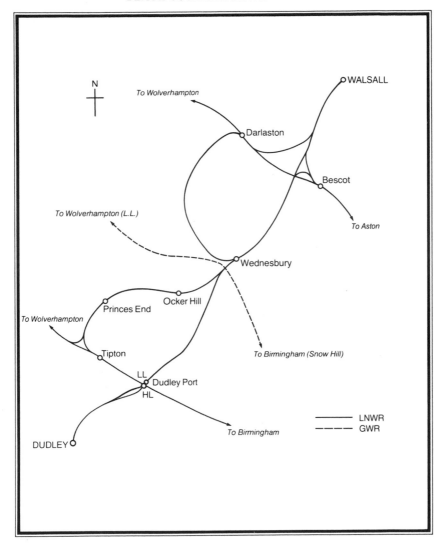

Between Dudley and Walsall, the South Staffordshire line was connected
with the Dudley Port (High Level) and Princes End branches and the Darlaston Loop

double track (down from James Bridge to Wednesbury) branched a succession of private sidings, including those to Horton & Son's nut and bolt works, Boys & Boden's James Bridge saw-mills, and those of the Darlaston Steel & Iron Company, shown in LNWR track diagrams as heading 'To Furnaces'.

The branch was busy for years, and it retained a toehold on the railway map at the beginning of 1983, still being worked, as it had been for many years, as a siding from Wednesbury ground frame. The section served the Patent Shaft works beside the A41. The branch trackbed is more accessible than some, a section through the centre of Darlaston being a public open space.

Princes End Branch

Closure of the Princes End branch was, to an extent, linked to the closure of Bilston steelworks. It was taken out of use, closed and subsequently lifted, after the last demolition trains had removed debris from the steelworks as the site was cleared. The rail economy removed an occasional distraction for Saturday morning shoppers at Gospel Oak, who had sometimes been able to watch a packed enthusiast special gingerly descending the 1 in 77–85 gradient towards Wednesbury.

From a three-car dmu forming the RCTS (Railway Correspondence and Travel Society) Reunion Railtour of November 1980, I saw pedestrians and motorists stop and watch our progress. The trackbed looked a shade precarious, perched on top of the embankment—'reputed to be on fire internally; certainly it is susceptible to subsidence,' to quote the railtour notes. The embankment was subsequently removed to try to quell the underground fires.

The branch lost another reason for its existence when Ocker Hill power station was virtually mothballed in the 1970s, another victim of the recession and changes in power generation.

Walsall–Anglesea Sidings

The next economy was complete closure of 5½ miles of the South Staffordshire between Walsall (Ryecroft Junction) and Anglesea sidings, still reached from Lichfield, in February 1984. The track has remained *in situ* to give planners the option of restoring passenger services to Lichfield from Walsall to meet a demand which could be created by extensive housing development taking place along the route, and for possible open-cast mining, similar to that on the adjacent Ryecroft–Cannock–Rugeley line.

The closure deprived Ryecroft Junction of another route and, subsequently, the quadrupled section between Walsall and the Junction, through a wide, twisting, climbing cutting with high brick retaining walls, was reduced to double track. Yet its capacity for freight services, and occasional passenger diversions, on the Rugeley and Sutton Park routes is still not overtaxed.

Requiem at Walsall

Walsall has had a string of stations. Perhaps the best known was that of 1923, with a semi-circular oak-panelled booking hall. It was demolished to make way for the multi-million-pound Saddlers Centre, built by the BR Property Board and a private developer and opened in 1980. It includes a small BR booking office for the town's last surviving passenger service, maintained by class 310 emus to Birmingham New Street via the Grand Junction route. They use a subterranean platform incorporated into the centre. Handy for shoppers. Raw, concrete – ugly in the extreme.

Walsall Local History Society claimed that the 1923 booking hall was the LNWR's compliment to Walsall 'as a town of tradition, self-respect and prosperity, with whom it was a great pleasure to do business'.

The Society's Local History Paper No. 3 *Walsall Stations*, first edition 1981, stated that if an awareness of the need for conservation could be created before it was too late, then the station (1923) would not have died in vain. 'The tones of its requiem will continue to vibrate.'

TOWN AND COUNTRY: *Plate 12 (above)* half the Stourbridge canal basin branch disappeared long ago, but Stourbridge Junction–Stourbridge Town remains open, with the distinction of being BR's shortest branch; *Plate 13 (below)* classic train of GWR clerestory coaches headed by a Pannier Tank on a Longbridge workmen's special crosses a classic viaduct: Dowery Dell, long demolished. Locomotive No 2718, 12 July 1935.

LNWR CONTRASTS: *Plate 14 (above)* Wednesbury Town. Its platforms on the South Staffordshire route were rarely as crowded as when an SLS special called. Class 8 2–8–0 No 48726 on middle line; *Plate 15 (below)* The LNWR atmosphere lingered on for years at Darlaston on the Grand Junction. On 13 August 1947 the 5.58pm Wolverhampton (High Level) – Walsall push-and-pull is powered by 2–4–2 tank No 6704.

CHAPTER 7

Coventry, Rugby, Leamington Spa

Coventry Avoiding Line

Six months after the German blitz on Coventry in 1940, in which 400 people were killed in one night, the *Railway Magazine* had a potted history of the Avoiding Line. It was opened, said the *Magazine*, chiefly to serve industrial premises on the west side of Coventry 'and is used for freight purposes only'.

> It is double track throughout, 3½ miles long, and has goods depots at Gosford Green on Birley Road, and Bell Green, on Stoney Stanton Road. The ruling gradient is 1 in 148, and some heavy constructional work was involved with embankments and cuttings of a maximum height and depth of 35ft and 31ft respectively.

By 1941—the *Railway Magazine* note was in the May issue—the avoiding line was still comparatively young: only twenty-seven years old, having been opened a few days after the outbreak of World War I. It was connected to the Foleshill Railway, from which guns were despatched for battleships and large cruisers being constructed for the Grand Fleet.

The line's decline began after the end of World War II, and it ceased to be a through route in 1963 when the junction on the main London & Birmingham line at Humber Road Junction was severed as a prelude to main-line electrification, the line being cut back to Gosford Green. Thousands of tons of material excavated during improvements at Birmingham New Street were dumped in Bell Green goods yard. They had to be moved again when private-car deliverers established a railhead there. Another was opened by another large firm at Gosford Green, but their life was comparatively short and Gosford Green finally became a Freightliner terminal. This, too, was open for only a short time.

If you want to catch a whiff of the flavour of the avoiding line, visit the trackbed soon for much of it is likely to disappear under a link road to the M6 and, presumably, satisfy some owners of the city's best-known products.

Rugby: junction of memories

My affection for the Rugby railway scene dates from spotting days in 1945, and sometimes as I pass through 'the barn'—for how else can the station be described?—I recall busy hours trying to 'cop' not only locomotives on the LNWR main line, but those that took you by surprise as they darted out of the cutting and on to the Great Central birdcage bridge and viaduct as they headed north. What problems were faced, and occasionally overcome: dying light, dirty engines, trains hidden behind each other as they passed, numbers of Great Central line locomotives above hidden by the steam of those below. Once I borrowed the modest family opera glasses, but this stage was too vast for them.

Reminders of those days are the birdcage bridge across the electrified main line, and two bridge abutments. The last time they had practical value in my life was when they supported track which took *Flying Scotsman* from Manchester via Sheffield to Marylebone on a Stephenson Locomotive Society / Manchester Locomotive Society special in April 1964. It was notable for *Flying Scotsman* being allowed through Woodhead tunnel, albeit piloted by an electric locomotive. In London, there was just time for a quick visit to Clapham Museum. I still lament the passing of Woodhead tunnel, Rugby viaduct

74

and Clapham Museum. The survivors of that year are *Flying Scotsman* and memories, stimulated for years by the vandalised shell of Rugby locomotive testing station, opened 1948.

It was a ghost of the age of steam that reappeared as I ran through Rugby on the APT during a test run at speeds which no Rugby-tested steam locomotive ever approached. The testing station shell was demolished in October 1984. A few weeks later, as if to lay steam's ghost, an APT made a record run between London and Glasgow in under 4 hours – halving steam's usual timings.

The Great Central main line is remembered in Volume 3 of this series, and Rugby's other lost line, to Leicester, is outside the compass of the present volume too. The single branch to Leamington Spa, along which I used to travel to spot, has proved durable carrying traffic to the Rugby cement works at Southam, on the Leamington Spa–Marton Junction–Weedon branch, thus keeping active a fragment of that rural switchback, which the LNWR once used to compete with Paddington for Leamington–London traffic.

Leamington Spa: LNWR

For years Leamington Spa was to me (and I know other enthusiasts) a powerhouse for railway knowledge. For many of the books and magazines on the shelves flanking my desk were dispatched from there by A. W. Pinder, a specialist and most helpful railway bookseller of many years' standing.

Leamington has always struck me as a place where, if anyone hated the Great Western Railway (not that I have heard of anyone who did), they could live without suffering too much transport inconvenience from such heresy. For they could use the LNWR to reach London and Birmingham, choosing from two routes: Kenilworth and Coventry, or Rugby (or Weedon, occasionally, for the service was not so frequent).

Although the Great Western with its main line and striking station was the dominant railway in Leamington for years,

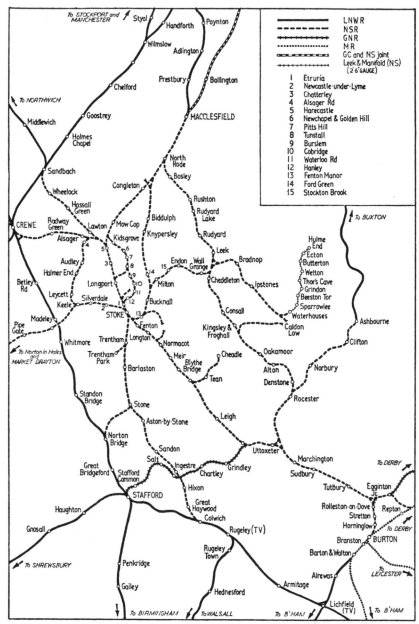

Taken from *A Regional History of the Railways of Great Britain, Vol 7: The West Midlands*, this map shows the North Staffordshire Railway, once described by a chairman as a 'small octopus'

it was not the first. The completion of the Coventry and War-wick line in December 1844 helped the Spa's expansion, and when the route effectively became a loop with the opening of the Rugby and Leamington branch in 1851, the Birmingham & Oxford main line was still 18 months away from opening. The North Western seemed happy when it did arrive for its official guide (1861 edition) noted of Leamington:

> Its continued prosperity is still further secured by the contiguity of the North Western and Great Western Railways. The traveller will scarcely find a more agreeable resting-place on his route than Leamington . . .

That contiguity lasted until the demise of the local system began in 1958, when the Weedon branch was closed to passengers, followed by that to Rugby—again operated by two-coach motor trains with veteran LNWR 2-4-2 tanks—only nine months later. The year 1965 saw the end of Birmingham services via the Kenilworth–Berkswell direct line, which avoided Coventry, and services to Coventry and Nuneaton.

For the next twelve years, Leamington residents could use only the Great Western routes to Birmingham and Paddington, but in 1977, the Coventry branch was re-opened to passengers, and while remaining mostly single, it was given Inter-City status, to feed long-distance expresses in and out of the new Birmingham International station, as well as Coventry.

London & North Western official guides of Victorian days analysed the two kinds of spa waters. With the famous travelling to the spa, Euston had to compete, and so it forced its own line through a built-up area of the town. Viaducts and bridges went up alongside the Birmingham & Oxford and did nothing to enhance the district. Had the rival companies agreed to use the same station and access lines through the town, Leamington would have been spared an ugly legacy of railway competition, which it bears to this day.

Beyond the narrow viaduct, the line headed into the quiet and pleasant countryside past the GWR Edwardian four-road

engine shed, which, together with carriage sidings, lay alongside the Birmingham & Oxford. When the shed and sidings
closed, land was made available for single-storey factories
close to the town centre, while not intruding on its historical
and elegant heart. To see that, you have to get off the train and
walk a short distance through parkland. Yet it is pleasant and
relaxing and makes Leamington a place where a search for lost
railways leads you to something more enjoyable, even if it
means the extra cost of buying a ticket which allows break of
journey.

Berkswell–Kenilworth–Leamington Spa

The LNWR's Leamington 'network' was completed in 1884
with the opening of a $4\frac{1}{4}$ mile direct line between Berkswell, on
the London & Birmingham, and Kenilworth, on the branch
from Coventry: the Coventry Avoiding Line (not to be con-
fused with the line of the same designation, which threaded the
western industrial area, page 73). The Berkswell route was
planned by Euston as an attractive and alternative competi-
tive route between Birmingham (New Street) and Leamington, in competition to that of the GWR from Birmingham
(Snow Hill).

Associated with the opening, was doubling between Lea-
mington and Kenilworth, though the Warwick & Leamington
Union of 1844 remained single between Kenilworth and
Coventry: Euston was forever suspicious of the aspirations of
Paddington, which even built a hotel in Coventry.

A station established $\frac{3}{4}$ mile north of Leamington Spa
Avenue had a variety of names, of which perhaps the most
explicit was Leamington Spa Milverton for Warwick. It lay on
the north side of Warwick New Road. The district name of
Milverton was also that, unofficially, of a six-road LNWR
locomotive shed called Warwick. It survived until 1958 and
for years it was the home of Webb 2–4–2 tanks which dominated the motor train services.

It was at Warwick (Milverton), rather than Avenue station,

78

that trains on the Rugby and Weedon branches terminated. The longest passenger link was via Weedon to Northampton (Castle), 35 miles of rolling, empty countryside, punctuated by only a few small towns and villages.

The Berkswell–Kenilworth line was never heavily used, but after the last passenger trains ran in 1965 it survived for freight for another four years, being a useful route keeping freight services between the West Midlands and South of England clear of Coventry. It became possible to do this in a different fashion after the 1966 opening of a new, north–south connection between the Western and Midland Region routes just north of Leamington Spa station. Its passenger potential was, of course, not exploited until 1977.

Today, at Berkswell, the branch trackbed leaves the London & Birmingham just south of a level-crossing and heads into the countryside, flanked by low hedges. More spectacular is the trackbed at Kenilworth. It curves away sharply north from the Coventry line and straight into a deep, overgrown cutting. Both ends of the branch can be viewed, and reflected upon, from the carriage window.

Perhaps the saddest part of railway history at Leamington was that while Euston and Paddington could not agree on the major issue of routes, they did manage to cooperate in small ways. For instance, the LNWR Time Tables (sic) of 1 October 1915 noted:

LEAMINGTON SPA – Between the Great Western and the L & N. W. stations, transfer porters are appointed to transfer luggage at a charge of 2d per article. The fares charged for through tickets do not include the transfer of luggage between the stations.

Leamington Spa was something of a LNWR byway. It was not possible to obtain pillows and rugs (at a charge of 6d, or 2½p, each) there, but they were available at Rugby, so one-way luxury, or at least extra comfort, was presumably available.

CHAPTER 8

The Midland Presence

The Stonebridge Railway

The Midland never imbued its system in the West Midlands with either the opulence it poured into St Pancras or the more restrained atmosphere of Derby station. This may have been partly a consequence of its presence at Birmingham New Street being so greatly overshadowed by that of the LNWR. Its best living memorial in the region must remain the Lickey Incline, while 6 miles of trackbed through undulating country-side just east of Birmingham will always have a place in rail-way history as those which carried rails which were part of a strategic main line for only three years.

They had their own individual identification as the Stone-bridge Railway because the route was authorised when it was promoted as a separate line by the Birmingham & Derby Junction in 1836 between Whitacre and Hampton. It completed a through route between Euston and Derby and was in effect a Birmingham cut-off for it enabled trains to avoid a journey via Stechford, where it was originally planned that the main lines from London and Derby should join.

The Stonebridge Railway achieved the distinction of being Britain's first downgraded main line. It happened in 1842, only three years after opening, when the B & DJ reached

Birmingham from Stechford, and other routes were opened between London and the North of England.

Far longer were the death throes of the Stonebridge Railway. The decline could be said to have set in in the 1860s when
the line was singled. It suffered mixed fortunes in both world
wars, losing its regular passenger trains from 1 January 1917.
By then the service was down to a single-coach train once each
way. Through goods were withdrawn in 1930, although the
northern half to Maxstoke was in use until 1939. For several
months in 1940–1, 2 miles north from Hampton were re-
opened when sand was urgently needed for airfield construction. Sand trains ran several times a week. The line was lifted
in 1951, yet despite the passage of time since then, interesting
remains can still be enjoyed: the original bow-window station
at Hampton, and the little engine shed which became a saw-
mill. It was once the headquarters of the locomotive superintendent of the Birmingham & Derby Junction, Matthew
Kirtley, who went on to reign at Derby until 1873.

The trackbed, minus its six rickety-looking bridges across
the river Blythe, is now bisected near Whitacre by the M6 and
the upgraded A45.

Birmingham Central Goods

The only other Midland branch to close in Birmingham – and
that was a dead-end – was the Central goods branch. But there
has been a major scaling-down of the Washwood Heath yards
to the east, where, as a boy, I was fascinated by the LMS Garratts, and the length of the sidings into which they disappeared
with their coal trains. Perhaps because I found no vantage
point from which to view the yards, I thought they were bigger
than they were. Now I know, and can tell you, they were of no
mean size. Washwood Heath coal yard alone could hold
almost 1,600 wagons and other sidings almost half as many.

As Curzon Street symbolises Birmingham's early railways,
Stanier House, multistoreyed, slimmer, less distinguished in
outline, is now the London Midland Region headquarters –

...UE.

MIDLAND

Every Monday, Wednesday, and Saturday
during JULY, AUGUST, and SEPTEMBER (except August 1st and 3rd); also on

Thursdays, July 9 & 23, Aug. 6 & 20, Sept. 3 & 17,
COOK'S CHEAP EXCURSION TICKETS BY EXPRESS TRAINS TO

CHELTENHAM
AND
GLOUCESTER

WILL BE ISSUED AS UNDER—

Times of starting and Third class fares there and back.

From	Day Trip. a.m.	Half-Day. p.m.		To CHELTENHAM. Day Trip.	Half-Day.	To GLOUCESTER Day Trip.	Half-Day.
Wolverhampton (High Level) ..	7 40	.....					
Willenhall (L. & N. W.)..	7 47	.....	}	**4/-**	..	**4/-**	..
Walsall	8 7	12 39					
Aldridge	8 15	12 47	}	**4/-**	**3/-**	**4/-**	**3/-**
Sutton Coldfield	8 27	12 59					
Saltley	8 17	1 19					
BIRMINGHAM (New St.)	9 35	1 52					
Camp Hill ..	9 14	1 14					
Moseley	9 7	1 8					
King's Heath	9 5	1 5	}	**3/6**	**3/-**	**4/-**	**3/-**
King's Norton	9 2	12 56					
Selly Oak	9 8	12 52					
Bournville	8 35	12 49					
Cheltenham .. arrive	10 29	2 50					
Gloucester ..	10 42	3 5					

Passengers from all Stations travel via Birmingham (New Street) in each direction.

Passengers return on day of issue as under—

For	From GLOUCESTER.			From CHELTENHAM.		
	Mons., Weds., and Thurs.	Sats., July 4, September 19 and 26.	Sats., July 11 to Sept. 12.	Mons., Weds., and Thurs.	Sats. July September 19 and 26.	Sats. July 11 to Sept. 12.
Willenhall & Wolverhampton (High Level) only	4 22 p.m.	4 22 p.m.	4 22 p.m.	4 36 p.m.	4 36 p.m.	4 36 p.m.
Other Stations..............	4 22 p.m. or 9 15 p.m.	4 22 p.m. or 8 57 p.m.	4 22 p.m. or 9 40 p.m.	4 36 p.m. or 9 31 p.m.	4 36 p.m. or 9 14 p.m.	4 36 p.m. or 9 56 p.m.

CONDITIONS OF ISSUE OF TICKETS.

CHILDREN under three years of age, free; three years and under twelve, half-fares.

NOTICE.—The tickets are not transferable, and will be available on the date of issue only, by the trains, and at the stations named; if used on any other date, by any other train, or at any other station than those named, the tickets will be forfeited, and the full ordinary fare charged.

The Company give notice that tickets for these excursions are issued at a reduced rate, and subject to the condition that the Company shall not be liable for any loss, damage, injury, or delay to passengers arising from any cause whatsoever.

No luggage allowed.

List of STATIONS, OFFICES, &c.,
OF THE
MIDLAND RAILWAY CO. and THOS. COOK & SON
WHERE TICKETS MAY BE OBTAINED.

MIDLAND RAILWAY CO.

WOLVERHAMPTON—High Level Station.
WALSALL—The Station.
BIRMINGHAM—New St. Station; "Swan" Office, New St.; 46, Snow Hill; 1, George St., Parade; 44, Hall St.; and 3, Edgbaston St.
And at the OTHER STATIONS shewn herein.
Handbills can also be obtained at BIRMINGHAM at the Midland Parcels Receiving Offices in various parts of the town.

THOS. COOK & SON.

WOLVERHAMPTON—22, Lichfield Street.
WALSALL—21, Park Street.
BIRMINGHAM—Stephenson Place; 52-54, Corporation Street; and 161, Soho Road.

TICKETS ISSUED ANY TIME IN ADVANCE.

Derby, June, 1914.

W. GUY GRANET, General Manager.

W.B. 85-1914. (3597.) Thos. Cook & Son, Printers, London and Birmingham.

Quickest and Most Comfortable Route between Birmingham, Bristol, Bath & WEST OF ENGLAND.

For Tourist and Shipping Information and Tickets call at Cook's Offices. Wolverhampton, Walsall, and Birmingham.

Cook's cheap excursions, summer 1914, including August 6 – two days after the outbreak of World War I. Did it run?

they moved from Euston House in spring 1985. But its roots lie in the past for it stands on the site of the Midland's Central goods depot in Suffolk Street, originally known as Worcester Wharf because of being canal served.

The depot was reached by a short branch from the Birmingham West Suburban Railway at Church Road Junction, Five Ways. It dropped under the Worcester & Birmingham Canal at 1 in 80.

Like Windsor Street and Soho Pool branches, the Midland's goods penetration into the city centre dated from the 1880s, being authorised in 1881 and opened in 1887. It had a shorter life than the others, closing in 1967. It was also smaller, its capacity of 375 wagons being below that of Camp Hill goods and coal yard, only a short distance south on the Derby–Bristol 'Direct' line.

Wolverhampton & Walsall Railway

Another Midland branch which ended life in two halves was the Wolverhampton & Walsall Railway, born in 1865 of a private company with offices at 57 Darlington Street, Wolverhampton. It was pro-LNWR since Euston had subscription powers. Its potential was local and limited because it was to serve towns where railways had been well established. The $6\frac{3}{4}$ route from the Stour Valley at Crane Street Junction, Wolverhampton, to Walsall (Ryecroft Junction), with the LNWR, opened in November 1872. In 1879, the line, which the LNWR had sold to the Midland three years earlier, achieved fresh status and traffic through the opening of the Wolverhampton & Midland Junction Railway from the Birmingham & Derby at Castle Bromwich, through Sutton Park on the leafy eastern outskirts of Birmingham, to Walsall, and junctions with the LNWR and the Wolverhampton route. The latter link was achieved by a Walsall avoiding line, which ran along a low hillside and crossed above the Rugeley and Lichfield lines and ran behind Ryecroft engine shed. The $\frac{3}{4}$ mile link is easy to trace, and the site of the shed is there too. Little remains, though air-raid shelters can be seen. They are rare relics in the railway scene today.

Midland trains bound from Walsall to Wolverhampton climbed a short, curved spur at Ryecroft, which joined the avoiding line at North Walsall Junction, close to a station of that name. Passenger trains were an early casualty of LMS administration, being withdrawn in 1931. For almost another forty years, the station, or its site, was passed by fuel trains bound for Birchills power station, about $\frac{3}{4}$ mile away, sustaining a claim that Ryecroft was Britain's last four-route junction.

The route was worked as two short branches from 1964 after the trackbed was severed by the M6 motorway builders. It was bisected at right angles near Pouk Hill (990998).

The most substantial monument to the Midland's presence in Wolverhampton is the squat and squarish Wednesfield Road goods depot (Midland), closed 1984, within sight of Wolverhampton station. It is easily spotted from the window of Stour Valley trains, while Birmingham–Wolverhampton expresses diverted via Bescot use the old Midland route between Crane Street and Heath Town Junctions: 30 chains of shallow S curves, which cross above the GWR tunnels at the southern approach to Low Level station. Rail access to that and the goods depot is via the electrically signalled Heath Town siding, effectively a shunting neck using the first stretch of the former Walsall branch.

The Midland's presence at Walsall was not confined to its Castle Bromwich–Wolverhampton route. Until 1925, it had a goods depot and locomotive shed between the station and Pleck Junction. The yard could stable 264 wagons – about 30 more than the LMS and GWR yards on the north side of the South Staffordshire route. For a time the 'Midland yard' was the Walsall Freightliner depot.

Brownhills Branch

A Saturday afternoon in April. Grey and cold. Dinghies race

across the choppy surface of Chasewater Lake. Outside the stoutly locked compound of the Chasewater Light Railway, I am warmed by memories flowing from a stack of old station nameboards I read through the wire fence. Rugeley (Trent Valley) Junction for Rugeley Town, Hednesford, Cannock and Walsall ... A girl trots past on a horse. She, too, looks cold.

But picture the scene on a summer's day. Dinghies with multicoloured spinnakers snatching a warm breeze; bright sunshine catching the steam of an 0–4–0 saddle tank pulling a diminutive six-wheel coach along a track following the water's edge.

By the time the Chasewater Light Railway came of age, it had been noted by the Ordnance Survey map-makers and accoladed as 'Rly Mus'—further welcome recognition for members of the railway preservation society who run it. For a line of only 2 miles, it has an interesting pedigree, being compounded of part of the Cannock Chase & Wolverhampton Railway of 1856, and an 1884 extension of the Midland's 4 mile branch to Brownhills from Aldridge on the Castle Bromwich–Walsall–Wolverhampton route.

Preserved industrial tank locomotives provide authentic historical atmosphere, for the Brownhills branch was the Midland's wedge into the Cannock Chase coalfield. It was essentially a mineral line serving several large collieries. Passenger trains were not introduced until more than two years after the branch opened in April 1882, and they were withdrawn in March 1930.

Branch closure followed the working-out of local pits in the 1960s. Gradually the line has been changed by local development. It is easy to trace from roads. In the centre of Walsall Wood, a bus stop at the junction of Coppice Road and Lichfield Road (A461) is often busier in an hour than Walsall Wood, which stood beside it, was in a week. Yet the Midland had built the station to last. Builders' specifications were for the eaves, gutters and rain pipes to be boiled in linseed oil; and coated with red oxide paint and, when positioned, by three coats of ordinary paint, more than ample protection from rain which drained into the gutters from locally made blue roof tiles. The station has long gone and rain brings renewed growth to grass sown on the in-filled trackbed.

CHAPTER 9

North Staffordshire

The Potteries Loop Line

'The Loop Line became ingrained in local folklore and is still remembered in the Potteries with respect and affection.' So wrote a London firm, Land Use Consultants, in a booklet prepared for the City of Stoke-on-Trent several years after the loop had closed.

Certainly, few workaday urban lines ever received the recognition of affection and importance that the novelist Arnold Bennett bestowed on the Loop. Yet its so-called immortality was local rather than national: it is unlikely that tourists ever asked for a Loop timetable so that they could include the area in their itinerary, for in Victorian days the Potteries were landmarked by coal and iron mines, and works which used these raw materials, not simply by the bottle-shaped kilns with which the area is perhaps most associated by people who never knew it.

If you ask for the equivalent of a Loop timetable today, the city council will send you a leaflet inviting you to explore *Routes of Fitness*. Route no. 1 is the Loopline Greenway, created as part of a multi-million-pound programme phased over fifteen years to turn pit landscapes, symbolised by huge spoil-heaps, large, deep and ugly clay-pits and disused railways, into public open spaces.

The Loop Greenway was designed as an access spine to open spaces: some, like suburban parks, already existing; others were projected new areas of recreation. The trackbed was designed by the planners as 'a country lane in a city'. So the Loop, which in life had been a barrier to pedestrian communication as it carved its way behind and over tightly packed streets, became a junction of walking routes.

Historically, the Loop was constructed slowly, being completed mainly between 1873 and 1875 to connect Stoke with: Hanley (the business and shopping centre of today); Burslem, the oldest of the Pottery towns; and Tunstall, an urban area which grew quickly in Victorian times. The towns merged, with Longton and Fenton, to form the city of Stoke-on-Trent in 1910.

Hanley, Burslem and Tunstall are now connected by the Loop Greenway, which stretches from Cobridge, north to Goldenhill.

The Loop's presence was even acknowledged by the London & North Western Railway, with whom the North Staffordshire Railway's relations were often touchy.

The Tourists' Picturesque Guide, 1876, noted a short branch from Etruria to Hanley (population 39,976), even though the Loop had by then just been completed to Kidsgrove.

> Scattered through the district are 260 pottery works, employing more than 10,000 hands, besides those earning wages in branches of manufacture which depend upon this industry, such as clay, colour, bone and flint-grinding etc.

In such ways did the Potteries prosper. Smoke thrown high by the small tanks that headed the Loop's strings of four-wheel carriage trains added more industrial grime, especially as much of the line was on heavy gradient. A clue to its highly individual character lay in such things as a note in timetables, which Arnold Bennett thought interesting enough to include in his writings, that 'The Loop Line service of trains runs at fixed intervals and is not in connection with other trains.'

WEDNESBURY'S CHANGING SCENE: *Plate 16 (above)* in late LMS days, Webb tank No 6661 calls at Wednesbury Town with a Walsall–Dudley train, a service withdrawn in July 1964; *Plate 17 (below)* Ten years later, a heavy coke train bound for Bilston Steelworks runs past the station remains, taking the Princes End branch. Locomotive No 37100.

PRINCES END (OCKER HILL) BRANCH: *Plate 18 (above)* a trip freight from Bescot Yard to Bilston Steelworks at the barrier crossing at Upper Church Lane, Princes End. Driver of Class 25 No 25138 is handing token to the signalman; *Plate 19 (below)* similar power Nos 25040 and 25069 for a DAA/DEG Marylebone–Euston railtour. It is passing the platform remains of Princes End station, closed 1916.

Closure of branches like the Loop threatened the area with further land dereliction and it did quickly become an 'eyesore', to quote the land consultants. Their report painted a vivid picture of its state at the time it was incorporated into Stoke's reclamation programme in 1968.

> The condition of the derelict sites was generally appalling—decaying station yards, weed-infested embankments, and everywhere the wastes of fly-tipping. For the community had historically turned its back on the railway as a source of noise and dirt; ten years' dereliction only strengthened this view and so encouraged fly-tipping and further deterioration of the environment. Physically the main problem was to clean up completely the railway lands, removing all the broken glass and tipped artefacts and to establish a reasonably tidy and maintainable surface.

Socially, said the planners, the problem was to project a new image for the line and earn public respect for the land after a decade of abuse and decay. Some bridges were demolished because they would cost too much to repair, but others were restored so that people could walk in safety without worrying about traffic.

Driving-wheels were positioned to mark the opening of the Pitt's Hill section of the trackbed in 1972, and, more ambitiously, the smokebox and chimney of GWR 2–8–0 No. 3817 did similar duty when Richard (now Lord) Marsh opened the Burslem section a year later. Now they are mileposts to remind generations who never knew the Loop of a busy, thriving, profitable railway, which helped to increase Victorian prosperity, perhaps by taking their great-grandfathers to and from work.

Harecastle Diversion

If the heart of the old Knotty is enshrined in trackbeds like the Loop, its living spirit is to be experienced in its best engineering achievements: two notable viaducts which carry the Stoke–Macclesfield main line high above rivers tumbling from Pennine flanks towards the Cheshire plain and the sea. Both are in Cheshire, although within sight of their owners' native

Staffordshire. They are companions, in an engineering sense, to three tunnels on a stretch of the main line, abandoned on electrification, through the Harecastle Ridge, watershed of Trent and Mersey. Because much of it was in tunnel or deep cutting, the stretch is different in substance and character from other NSR remains.

The Ridge sorely troubled canal promoters, Brindley taking eleven years to pierce it with the Trent & Mersey Canal. His work, hailed as masterful on completion in 1777, was soon congested and was duplicated by Telford only half a century later. His tunnel survives, but today's rail route through the Ridge is comparatively new: the concrete-lined tunnel of only 220yd is still whitish. It is the main feature of the Harecastle Diversion (the official title), which was taken through a shallow, green and wooded valley just west of the original line from Chatterley sidings, near Longport, to Kidsgrove.

Engineers surveying an electrified route between Euston and the North West found that, in addition to the ravages caused by steam locomotives blasting their way through for more than a century, the tunnels were too narrow for modern stock. Harecastle North tunnel (130yd) was opened out; and the Middle (180yd) and South (1,763yd) tunnels, and the deep cutting which separated them, were abandoned, leaving the old NSR network without a tunnel more than a mile long. Despite the company having penetrated several hilly districts, there were only thirteen in all.

In daylight it is easy to spot both ends of the Diversion from the carriage window. The line curves away from the original route near Chatterley sidings, a mostly grassy wilderness, pinpointed by a few sidings, and returns to the original alignment through the opened-out, cross-braced cutting that was once North tunnel. The northern portal of the Middle tunnel is visible, tucked away in an overgrown cutting on the Up side of the Diversion, which opened on 27 June 1966.

A good place from which to get the feel of lines old and new is a wide road running between Tunstall and the A500. This route crosses the Diversion close to

Chatterley sidings and the south portal of South tunnel.

Talke and Chesterton Branches

Chatterley sidings were also a junction, for they were largely fed by two mineral branches which climbed the Harecastle Ridge to Talke and Chesterton, where there were several large collieries, and tile and chemical works.

> The writer can recall, in the 1920s, seeing this train at Chatterley, on more than one occasion, but always behind rows of wagons, so that only the long chimney, the top of the saddletank, the shapely brass safety valve cover and the cab of the Talke engine could be seen.

This passage is a quotation from J. R. Hollick, doyen of NSR historians, recalling the frustrations of trying to spot the daily goods carrying coal-tar products from Talke to Bradwell chemical works in the valley below. It was worked by a privately owned engine, for the Talke branch was among many on which the NSR allowed private firms to run their own locomotives and trains.

In 1904, the NSR had bought 1 mile 55 chains of the branch after leasing it for some forty years from Ralph Sneyd, owner of local collieries and ironworks. Despite its short length, the branch qualified for inclusion by the NSR in its annual entries in the *Railway Year Book*: 'The steepest gradient on a goods or mineral line is 1 in 36 for a distance of 40 chains at Red Street, Talk-o'-th'-Hill, falling towards Chatterley.'

Chesterton was originally a branch off that to Talke, stemming from Chesterton Junction. It was a hugely successful branch and like its parent never carried passengers. The junction was abolished in 1877, and afterwards the branches ran parallel downhill to Chatterley sidings. Although both were born in the 1860s, the Chesterton proved far the healthier, for while Talke died slowly from 1931, its neighbour survived until 1968, finally serving Parkhouse colliery, reached through a back-shunt needed to conquer the gradient. Although the pit was nearly worked out, the north-facing junction was abolished when the Harecastle Diversion was constructed, and the approach turned south, running alongside the Down main line to Bradwell sidings at Longport.

Audley Mineral Lines

In 1931, the LMS instructed Henry Blacklock & Company to delete the passenger timetable in *Bradshaw's* of the Alsager–Keele service. It was a request with which the printers were becoming increasingly familiar. They had already deleted another Alsager service—that over the Sandbach branch—the previous year, and the Biddulph Valley passenger trains three years before that.

The Audley service ended because of competition from buses which ran over routes more direct and convenient for local people. But the branch, opened in 1870 to serve several large pits, was, in the early 1930s, far too busy for its rails to go rusty. Indeed, coal trains continued for another three decades, closure occupying several years in the 1960s in step with the working-out of the pits. Leycett's small station was demolished in 1969, with the rest of the village, when miners were rehoused in Silverdale and Madeley. The Audley branch trackbed is easy enough to trace, although between Audley and Alsager a short section succumbed to the bulldozers preparing the route of the A500 link road between the M6 and the Potteries.

At Alsager, in 1982, the shell of the former LMS shed (5E) still stood beside the Crewe line and East Junction, where the Audley line curved sharply south to cross a busy suburban road. Low abutments, flanked by trackbed, remain.

The Audley Mineral Lines was a collective title, embracing several other short, once busy, branches: Chesterton (page 93), Audley, Bignall Hill, Jamage and the Grange branch. Because the Potteries are the graveyard of these and a number of privately owned mineral lines, I have had to be selective rather than exhaustive. The history of the former NSR branches is detailed in my history of that company: Rex

94

Christiansen and R. W. Miller, *The North Staffordshire Railway* (David & Charles, 1971).

Alsager–Sandbach

It is pleasant to explore the 6½ mile branch which for more than a century meandered north-west between the market towns of Alsager and Sandbach. It passed through some six miles of quiet South Cheshire countryside well off the beaten tourist track, where it is easy to relax. But the task is not quite as rewarding as it once was, for the branch has made two contributions to enhance preserved railways elsewhere.

On the morning of Saturday 18 November 1978, enthusiasts of the North Staffordshire Railway Society added their own piece of history to Sandbach, a town steeped in the stuff, by transporting the retired sixteen-lever signal-box from Elton crossing to Cheddleton, where it now leads a more active life. The route of the transporter was through the centre of Sandbach, which meant that the box got closer to the town's heart than the trains which it controlled ever did.

For the branch, pursuing its course to the Manchester–Crewe main line by the station, got no closer to the town centre than Wheelock, a village a mile to the south. The branch reached Ettiley Heath on the southern outskirts of Sandbach in 1852, and waited fourteen years to join the London & North Western. Local passenger services did not begin for another twenty-seven years (1893) and are historically notable for their brevity.

For the LMS anticipated Dr Beeching by more than thirty years, ending them in 1930, though the branch continued to have a useful life as a Crewe avoiding route for freight and oil trains until the early 1970s.

You will find another of its little signal-boxes, from Hassell Green, being well looked after in West Cheshire: at Hadlow Road station, a showpiece of the Wirral Country Park, created from the former Hooton–West Kirby branch. The box is kept company by its level crossing gates. They now flank the

B5151 at Willaston, the village the station served.

Churnet Valley

Goods trains of a length and weight allowed only in wartime, laboriously pounding the Churnet Valley route on a wild and snowy night in 1944, are part of an indelible memory of the first night I spent away from home. I was alone: the only member staying in an old hall that was Rudyard Youth Hostel. Stout wooden doors creaked on ancient hinges and the wind whistled through the building with its stone floors as I snuggled into a lower bunk in an empty dormitory. Then, the eerie noises were overpowered by others: passing trains. How comforted I felt.

The memories can never be repeated, for much of the line which I crossed as I cycled deeper into Staffordshire the next morning has long gone. The Churnet Valley provided the shortest route between Euston and Manchester (London Road), and although it was used by some through services, the majority ran via Stoke or Crewe, not least because they were faster routes. Of the Churnet Valley, 9 miles at each end have been lifted: between North Rode and Leek Brook Junction, and from Oakamoor (British Industrial Sand) sidings and Uttoxeter. The now singled Leek Brook–Oakamoor section remains busy. It includes the section of line that runs through what is sometimes, rather exaggeratedly, termed the Staffordshire Rhineland, and also the small wayside station, strikingly Tudor in design, at Cheddleton, which is preserved and living as the headquarters and evocative museum of the North Staffordshire Railway Society.

Some passengers never forgot their journeys through the Churnet Valley. Among them was Mr J. E. Coates who wrote from Bath, at the age of eighty-seven, 'as one born (1883) and brought up in Oakamoor'. From 1896 to 1901 he travelled to Uttoxeter Grammar School:

The 8am Oakamoor to Uttoxeter collected schoolboys on the way.

The carriages were without corridors, lighted (?) by dim oil lamps, and heated (?) by battered footwarmers.

I remember the excursions from Oakamoor and neighbouring stations, often starting about 4am. A favourite was to Belle Vue, Manchester; others were to Blackpool and Llandudno.

Today, there are occasional excursions to and from Cheddleton, reversing at Leek Brook. Apart from Cheddleton, two other stations are preserved. Rushton is a private house and Alton Towers, three-storeyed to match the main estate building, is a Listed Building. It was sold by BR to Staffordshire County Council, and has been restored by Landmark, a non-profit-making charity, which acquired it from the county council for a nominal sum.

Guidebooks, including those which tell the story of continuing volunteer enterprise at Cheddleton, are what you need now, rather than timetables, to enjoy the Churnet route. Steep, wooded hillsides robbed the rail travellers of yesterday of the chance to appreciate much of the beauty of the scenery through which they were passing. Today's walkers will experience no such frustration, for line closure helped local authorities to provide more access to the countryside, and so you find sections of trackbed which they have borrowed in a comprehensive guide, published by Staffordshire County Council, called *The Staffordshire Way: Mow Cop to Rocester*. The Way itself is to stretch for 90 miles south to Kinver Edge.

Dropping down from Mow Cop ridge, the walker intent on following the Guide's 32 miles to Rocester will first meet the Biddulph Valley trackbed (page 101), before climbing to the Cloud, a round hill some 600ft above sea-level, which dominates the northern mouth of the Churnet valley. For years it was a grandstand from which to spot the smoke trails of mainline expresses between Stoke and Macclesfield, and the more sedate and leisurely ones of the Churnet Valley local services. They often fell away as drivers braked to 20mph at North Rode Junction. Double whistles called for in the LMS Sectional Appendix alerted you to their presence if you were picnicking and eyes were on tasty food rather than scenery.

North Staffordshire Railway

Commencing Monday, November 22nd and until December 24th inclusive, NEW TRAINS

WILL RUN BETWEEN

UTTOXETER and
KINGSLEY AND FROGHALL

As Under:

	a.m			a.m.
Uttoxeter	dep. 5 30	Kingsley & Froghall	dep. 6 10
Rocester	,, 5 40	Oakamoor	,, 6 16
Denstone	,, 5 43	Alton	,, 6 21
Alton	,, 5 49	Denstone	,, 6 27
Oakamoor	,, 5 54	Rocester	,, 6 31
Kingsley & Froghall	arr. 6 0	Uttoxeter	arr. 6 39

THIRD CLASS

Weekly Workmen's Tickets

available up to the following Saturday Night, will be issued at the undermentioned fares :—

Rocester & Froghall	and Back	-	4/-
Denstone & Froghall	,,	-	3/6
Alton & Froghall	,,	-	2/-
Oakamoor & Froghall	,,	-	1/3
Rocester & Oakamoor	,,	-	2/6
Denstone & Oakamoor	,,	-	2/-
Alton & Oakamoor	,,	-	9d.
Froghall & Oakamoor	,,	-	1/3

These Tickets will be available on the Outward Journey by any Train due at the Station to which the Ticket is available at or before 9 35 a.m., and on return by any Train at or after 3 30 p.m., except on Saturdays when they will be available by any Train after 12 o noon.

CONDITIONS UPON WHICH THE TICKETS ARE ISSUED.

WORKMEN'S TICKETS are issued at a reduced rate, and in consideration thereof the Ticket is accepted by the Passenger on the express condition that the liability of the Company to make compensation for injury or otherwise in respect to the Passenger shall be limited to a sum not exceeding ONE HUNDRED POUNDS, and that the amount of compensation payable in respect of any such Passenger shall, subject to such limitation, be determined by an Arbitrator to be appointed by the Board of Trade and not otherwise. Also that no claim shall be made by reason of the late running of the Trains named. The Tickets are not Transferable or available for Passengers to break their journey at intermediate Stations.

The Tickets, which must be produced each morning and night to be nipped, and given up on Saturday, when demanded by a Servant of the Company, will be forfeited if used by any but the authorised Trains, as specified above, and the holder charged the Full Ordinary Fare.

Railway Offices, Stoke-on-Trent, November, 1915.   **W. D. PHILLIPPS, General Manager.**

Sherwin & Co. (Hanley), Ltd., Foundry Street Printing Works, Hanley.

In a wartime winter: extra workmen's trains through the Churnet Valley.
Cheap fares, but maximum accident compensation limited to £100

The Cloud overlooked—and still does—a notable viaduct on which the local trains—an LMS parallel-boiler 2–6–4 tank and four non-corridor coaches, as I remember them—came into clear view.

The Staffordshire Way reaches their trackbed ¾ mile north of the preserved gothic station at Rushton, and continues past it for a similar distance, before taking to the hillside west of Rudyard Lake (2 miles by ¾ mile), created as a reservoir for the Macclesfield Canal, and from which Kipling was given his Christian name. His father, a Stoke architect, had proposed to his mother beside the lake.

The guidebook shows the trackbed following the eastern shore as a disused railway walk; its designation would have been different if the first enthusiasts who wanted to bring steam back to the valley had been successful. For the Cheshire & Staffordshire Railway Society wanted a steam link between a picnic area, proposed by the county council near the lake, and Leek, only 2 miles to the south. But, as J. L. Roberts, its publicity officer, explained in 1973:

> Unfortunately, Leek Urban Council failed to see the amenity value of this project, despite the support of 1,000 Leek citizens who signed a petition supporting the Society's aims. The station is now demolished to make way for a sewer scheme.
>
> The Society, however great this setback may seem, has decided to investigate the feasibility of re-opening another stretch of the picturesque Churnet Valley Railway line, between Oakamoor and Alton.

So Cheddleton came about. Meanwhile, five years later steam did return to the trackbed at Rudyard, but only for a short time. The Leek & Manifold Railway, a 10¼in system scaled down to one third of the size of its modest namesake, was established on a stretch of just over ½ mile, south from Rudyard station picnic area. It was the initiative of Waterhouses Secondary School, led by the ambition and financial drive of the deputy headmaster, Brian Nicholson. He spent thousands of pounds having two L & M replica locomotives built, while pupils worked on coaches for 120 passengers. The railway opened on 27 June 1978—seventy-four years to the day on which the Leek & Manifold had opened. There were hopes that the narrow-gauge line might be extended along the entire east bank of Rudyard Lake, but it closed only two years later when Mr Nicholson moved from Waterhouses.

The stretch between Rudyard and Leek is walkable to the northern outskirts of Leek, short of the tunnel which had its southern portal in a deep cutting north of the station.

The living railway occupies the most attractive parts of the valley, past Cheddleton to Oakamoor, where there is a picnic site at the start of another section of officially walkable trackbed, extending almost 3 miles to Denstone, though this is not part of the Staffordshire Way, which is close-by, to the west. From Denstone, the Way takes to the fields towards Rocester, crossing the Ashbourne branch (see below) on the outskirts of the village.

South of Denstone there is plenty to interest the seeker of old railways who tires of rural surrounds. The trackbed is traceable almost to Rocester, where the site of the station demolished in summer 1970, and the Ashbourne branch junction, were swallowed into the extensive, landscaped grounds of J. C. Bamford Excavators. And at Spath, on the northern outskirts of Uttoxeter, the B5030 was crossed by Britain's first automatic half-barrier level-crossing, installed on 5 February 1961. It is not far from a later one at Hixon on the Colwich–Stoke line—a point noted in the report of the public inquiry—the first of its kind since the Tay Bridge disaster of 1879—into an accident on 6 January 1968. Eleven people were killed and forty-five injured when a Manchester–Euston express hit a heavy transporter carrying a 120 ton transformer, which had got stuck on the half-barrier crossing.

Rocester–Ashbourne

Victorian tourists who bought Baddeley's *Guide to the Peak District* in 1894 would have found this advice:

Visitors from the south will do well to make Ashbourne or Matlock their starting-point, remembering that the routes to Ashbourne or Dovedale, from Rocester or Alton, are worth a much more close exploration than can be made from the window of a railway carriage.

From Rocester, the Ashbourne branch followed the south bank of the Dove. It opened in 1852 and assumed added importance when the LNWR completed its branch south from Buxton in 1899 and began somewhat sparse services between London and Manchester via Buxton. But the Ashbourne branch of the NSR is recalled as a local line, trains to and from Uttoxeter taking just under half an hour for 11½ miles with three stops. Four trains ran on weekdays, two carrying through coaches for Buxton. For Saturday markets, cheap tickets were issued to Ashbourne from eight NSR stations, including Derby and Stoke.

Horse-boxes and carriage trucks were attached to many local trains. On 18 February 1899—eighty-five years to the week before I wrote this section—Farmer Perkins sent five calves from Ashbourne to Uttoxeter. They travelled in horse-box No. 08, according to the faded brown 'Counterfoil of Way-bill for Carriages, Show Vans or Caravans, Luggage &c., Horses, Cattle, Asses, Mules, Dogs, and other Quadrupeds, and for Poultry and other Live Birds by Passenger Train.'

Biddulph Valley

While the Potteries Loop carried a passenger service individual and intensive enough to give it a measure of immortality, the Biddulph Valley branch just east over the Turnhurst Ridge, did not carry regular services until four years after its opening in 1860, and even then they were sparse. And it lost them as early as 1927. For years there were proposals to link the lines, making the Biddulph Valley branch 'a valuable northward extension of the Loop', to quote Dr Hollick. The Turnhurst line was to have taken its name from the hall that provided a home for the canal engineer

James Brindley (born 1716) until his death in 1772.

Brindley's drive and imagination in canal building proved no inspiration to the Turnhurst promoters, who only managed to drive survey pegs along their route. Some remained in the ground for more than half a century, Dr Hollick noting that those between Turnhurst and Pitts Hill survived until the 1930s.

But the Biddulph Valley promoters were assured of success from completion, and the diabolically small print of *The Railway Times* hailed the branch as 'inaugurating a new era in the development of the vast mineral wealth with which the district abounds'.

Its pits included Chatterley Whitfield, which in 1900 became Britain's first to produce a million tons a year. How coal trains must have rolled. The pit closed in 1977 and with it went another short stretch of the branch. It ceased to be a through route when the Manchester–Stoke line was prepared for electrification, the northerly outlet, rising over a north-facing spur from Congleton Lower Junction to Upper, being closed in December 1963. Five years later, the 1 mile Brunswick branch, which formed the northern tip of the line at Congleton, closed, together with the section from Congleton Lower to Victoria Colliery, Black Bull. That was followed by Victoria Colliery–Chatterley Whitfield (now, incidentally, a living mining museum, where visitors can descend 700ft underground). The stretch from the colliery to Ford Green followed in 1976 and the last stretch, to the Stoke–Leek Brook line at Milton, in 1979. The scene was set for a major programme of land reclamation to improve the once blighted environment and provide more open space for recreation. The results have been good.

The Mow Cop Trail occupies nearly 2 miles of trackbed on the eastern outskirts of Congleton. It passes close to where the branch burrowed under the Macclesfield Canal—a section that is a local footpath (881625). A county council leaflet, *Exploring Cheshire's Eastern Fringe*, is handy and interesting, noting that, since closure, the branch has become a haven for wildlife, has a great variety of flowers, over sixty species of birds and many butterflies, all of which enjoy its sheltered cuttings.

Municipal and commercial authorities in the Potteries are still concerned that people who do not know the area regard it as black, bleak, industrial and smoky. Converting industrial branches like the Biddulph into walkways helps visitors—and local residents—to discover for themselves just how pleasant and peaceful are many areas from which industry—and railways—have gone.

But in fact, a stretch of the Biddulph branch remains among the busiest freight lines in the Potteries, for it is part of the route to Caldon quarry and Oakamoor sand terminal. This is because the Biddulph branch was always regarded as running 12½ miles from Stoke Junction (with the Derby line) via Milton Junction (3½ miles east), where the single line turned north into the Valley. The junction was not created until Stoke and Leek Brook Junction were linked in 1867. Two of the Biddulph branch original stations, Fenton Manor and Bucknall, continued to be used by Stoke–Leek trains until 1956.

Longton Adderley Green & Bucknall Railway

Since 1964 the lost railways have included a 3½ mile mineral branch which left the Biddulph Valley at Botteslow Junction and ran south-east to serve areas from which it accurately took its title. It opened in 1875 on the initiative of coal owners to serve a string of mines, large and small, including five owned by the Chatterley Whitfield company. It was taken over in 1895 by the North Staffordshire Railway, the Act including powers for the abandonment of a ¼ mile section near the southern end, Millfield Junction on the Stoke–Derby main line. The object of splitting the branch was to allow the NSR to obtain higher revenue from longer hauls of the output of the pits. The branch was steeply graded at up to 1 in 48 and the break made to simplify operating. Powers to run passenger trains were obtained but never used, and the two ends became light railways after the passing of the 1896 Act.

The line remained busy until the collieries were worked out and closed, and the branch closed in the mid 1960s. It has since been obliterated, a stretch of trackbed to Fenton Road at Bucknall becoming a footpath.

Stoke-on-Trent–Market Drayton

Once, heaven was a sunny strip enclosed between a stout wooden fence and the track of the West Coast main line alongside Whitmore troughs, south of Crewe. A lineside photographic permit was my passport to a grassy bank, several miles long, which I thought quite as sacred as any cricket pitch. Memory has sharpened the contrast of the setting where I spent happy days recording the last years of steam, which still hauled every express apart from the *Royal Scot*, then in the hands of experimental diesels with white overalled footplate crews.

But while the four tracks were always busy, the Stoke–Madeley branch was hardly used. Few trains puffed out of cuttings flanking the main line, ran across a low embankment and an unprepossessing bridge across the mighty route below and then disappeared again. For the Madeley spur, between main line and branch, was still several years in the future. It was only in 1962, when diesels had far greater command of expresses, that coal trains began climbing the spur and reversing, further animating the Madeley railway scene.

They still run the 4 miles between there and Silverdale and Holditch collieries at Newcastle, part of a merry-go-round circuit to Ironbridge power station. Reversal at Madeley has been under control of the main-line box since the closure in 1971 of Madeley Chord box, on the embankment above, only five years after opening.

The run-round loop stops within sight of where Madeley Road station once stood. It was so isolated that it closed in 1931—a quarter of a century before Stoke–Market Drayton trains stopped running beyond Silverdale, which remained the

branch passenger terminus until 1964. I came across the vandalised shell of Madeley Road station buildings shortly before
their demolition in the early 1960s. They were tucked into a
hillside, 2 miles south of Madeley village and within sight of
the West Coast main line. I thought that the station house
could have been a snug place to live if you liked quiet (apart
from passing trains): an enthusiast's rural bolt hole, perhaps.

Retention of the Silverdale–Madeley section of the branch
meant bridging the M6 motorway, which was constructed
through the area in 1961, and today drivers find a single-line
bridge, impressively high, spanning six lanes of a steeply
sloping stretch of the motorway just north of Keele services.
The western end of the railway bridge is close to the site of
Keele station. It has reinforced concrete beams 297ft long,
thought to be the longest of their kind when they were constructed. Because the bridge is flanked by cuttings, the motorway driver gets only a fleeting glimpse of the pleasant
countryside west of the Potteries, though the searcher for the
branch remains can enjoy it.

Trentham Branch

Sit back and remember the Trentham branch in armchair
comfort. For that is virtually the only way you can do so,
because the trackbed has been obliterated. The NSR opened
the branch in Edwardian days to encourage people to enjoy
Trentham Gardens, which surrounded the Hall built by the
Dukes of Sutherland, and abandoned by them in 1905 because
of the smelly Trent nearby. Most of the Hall was subsequently
demolished, but the gardens remain and are open to the
public. It is nearly thirty years since the last excursion train
ran in 1957, and modern houses fringing an estate now stretch
almost to the Stoke–Stone section of the main line, although
the site of the pretty, ornate Trentham station (in keeping with
the architecture of the Hall) remains green. Beside two main-
line platforms, Trentham station had one for the branch.

On OS maps prior to closure, the station's main-line

platforms were marked by a red circle, that of the branch in white, because it had been long closed.

For more than twenty years, a striking monument to the virtual end of railway building in the Potteries lay across the A34, London Road, just beyond the branch terminus. It was a steel girder bridge on high brick abutments. It was to have carried the Newcastle-under-Lyme & Silverdale Light Railway. This was authorised as a 4 mile extension of the Pool Dam branch to form a southern loop. Construction was delayed by the advent of World War I and when World War II broke out, the bridge was a small, yet useful, source of desperately needed scrap metal.

Housing development has changed the character of the Trentham area from rural to urban. Just how rural it once was can be detected from the date of the closure of Hanford Road Halt, the only intermediate stop on the 1¼ mile branch—1913. Regular passenger services were another casualty, like the bridge, of World War II, closing a few days after its outbreak. Excursions continued, the last one being worked by a dmu.

Cold Meece Branch

'There are many places near to Stone well worth a visit,' stated the NSR's guide, *Picturesque Staffordshire*, in 1908, and it placed Swynnerton village foremost amongst them. That was in 1908 when Stone was the nearest station. Thirty years later, Swynnerton got one of its own, well almost—for it never appeared in public timetables even though it was used by 3 million passengers a year. For it was an allegedly secret munitions factory, allegedly since it was sometimes mentioned by the Germans in broadcasts by Lord Haw-Haw. The branch serving it opened in August 1941, running from the Norton Bridge–Stone line at Swynnerton Junction, nearly 1½ miles, and fanning out into four long, corrugated-iron-roofed platforms: a Trentham branch on a grand, contrastingly ugly scale.

When the veil of secrecy was lifted, the branch found a champion in the late Hugh Oliver, born in the Potteries, but

LEAMINGTON BOUND: *Plate 20 (above)* Berkswell–Kenilworth, the Coventry Avoiding Line. A Birmingham (New Street)–Leamington Spa train, headed by Compound No 1122 passing Berkswell Down Distant Signal on 12 May 1948; *Plate 21 (below)* last regular Rugby–Leamington local train leaving Marton behind tank No 41227, 15 June 1959.

PROMOTED AND RELEGATED: *Plate 22 (above)* now part of the Inter City network, for years Leamington Spa–Coventry was a branch line in passenger terms. No 41228 passes Kenilworth Junction in 1957. The Berkswell branch diverges behind the signal box; *Plate 23 (below)* Aldridge, on the extant Walsall–Castle Bromwich route. The station closed to passengers when local services were withdrawn in 1965. It was the junction for the Brownhills branch, also Midland, from which passenger services were withdrawn in 1930.

who wrote of its lines from his North London home. He also chronicled the Trentham and other branches.

After closure, the station site was developed by government departments for a variety of uses, including vehicle testing, while the equipment was sold in July 1969. It was listed as: 'Rails, concrete and wooden sleepers, chairs, fishplates, points, etc., a steel railway bridge and railway weighbridge.' Track, in the same single lot, extended to about $8\frac{3}{4}$ miles. Such was the extent of the secret web.

Leek & Manifold Light Railway

The Leek & Manifold Light Railway has run into more controversy in the half century since closure in 1934 than it encountered in the mere thirty years of its existence. The trackbed's conversion into a walkway soon after closure, amid much official celebration in an era when such happenings were rare, pleased many country lovers who found they had a delightful valley which they could explore in peace and at leisure. But hard-surfacing the trackbed incensed many people who felt that city pavements had been laid in glorious countryside.

The planning authority of the Peak National Park regards the route as a pleasant place to direct school parties and walkers, primarily to take pressure off the better-known Dovedale, only 2 miles east.

Concern for the peace and quiet of the Manifold Valley led to anger when Waterhouses Secondary School announced plans to revive a railway—a $10\frac{1}{4}$ in gauge replica. It was to run $1\frac{3}{4}$ miles between Grindon and Wetton. Attitudes quickly hardened. 'I do not see why the valley should be for a privileged few,' Brian Nicholson, the deputy headmaster, was quoted as saying in 1973. But protesters, including ramblers, felt the valley was congested at summer weekends. One objector wrote to a local paper suggesting Blackpool as a better venue. Pupils at the school took their own opinion poll—and found that over 98 per cent of local people supported their application to the Peak Park Planning Board. But the board members did not vote that way and the railway was launched at Rudyard (page 99).

There was little opposition and a lot of encouragement when the original railway was suggested. One engine in steam was the mode of operation throughout its entire life. If the company's second engine was steamed simultaneously, they worked double-headed for their depot at Hulme End, at the upper end of the route. The basic weekday passenger service was three trains, with summer extras, when tourists were sometimes packed into open wagons. Trains were generally mixed, and they included narrow-gauge transporter wagons carrying standard-gauge milk and other wagons. They were among the highly successful inventions of the line's engineer, E. R. Calthrop, a notable narrow-gauge railway expert with a worldwide reputation.

The Leek & Manifold trackbed had been given by the LMS, after only eleven years of ownership, to Staffordshire County Council on 23 July 1937—less than a month after the LMS had made bigger headlines with the *Coronation Scot* trials, when it approached within sight of Crewe at 113mph. Surfacing the light-railway trackbed cost the county council £6,000, and far more was spent converting the 1½ miles between Redhurst and Butterton, including Swainsley tunnel (154yd), into a single-track road with passing places.

The L & M continues to be the best documented of all NSR lines. Among the most recent of a number of books is one by Keith Turner (David & Charles, 1980). Several of its illustrations show what visitors will find today.

Waterhouses Branch

Steam did not totally retreat when the little engines dropped their fires in March 1934, for passenger trains continued to Waterhouses until autumn of the following year. Did ramblers feel sad that they could no longer get into the valley in fascinating and leisurely comfort provided by the little coaches?

Meanwhile a goods service continued to Waterhouses until 1943. And to this day there is a strong rail presence in the area, for several-times-daily trains to Caldon quarry still pass the site of Caldon Junction, where the Waterhouses trains diverged.

Burton upon Trent–Tutbury

Writing this section has given me the pleasure of taking from my bookshelves *Bradshaw's Guide* for November 1946 to recall, from page 530, a Sunday journey I made to Burton for an organised visit to local railways and the Midland shed, where outside-frame locomotives were to be found. I must have caught the 11.25am 'Tutbury Jennie'—two LMS compartment coaches and a Midland 0–4–4 tank, allowed 12min for the $5\frac{1}{4}$ miles. This was 2min less than on weekdays when a service of nine trains spaced over 13½ hours also served three intermediate stations: Rolleston-on-Dove (the river here not quite as striking as in the hills further north), Stretton & Clay Mills and Horninglow.

Burton was once enmeshed by railway lines, main, branch and industrial: Bass, the brewers, had a private system that grew to 17 miles. Its spirit is now encapsulated in a section of the Bass Museum, open seven days a week.

The Tutbury Jennie—no one knows how or why it got its cheery nickname—was not the most important service on the NSR's Burton branch. That honour belonged to goods, not only those of the NSR, but of the Great Northern, owners of the Egginton–Dove Junction spur. It used running powers from 1878 to reach its own goods station in Burton, introducing passenger services from Nottingham (37 miles) three months later.

The NSR was destined to serve Burton for 120 years from 1848. Economies were spread over nineteen years, an inordinate length of time considering how short the branches were, beginning with the closure of the three intermediate stations in 1949—eleven years ahead of withdrawal of the Tutbury Jennie. So it ended its life as something of a local flyer.

Stafford & Uttoxeter Railway

On a summer's day in 1879, Mr Ridley, of the North Stafford-shire Railway's Rocester station, acknowledged receipt of a circular from the Accountant's Department at Stoke-upon-Trent (sic). It gave Mr Ridley, addressed without Christian name or initial, authority to accept Stafford County Prison Warrants: 'The above, signed by Major Fulford, the Governor of the Prison, may in future be accepted by you and remitted to the Bank as Cash, and dealt with in the same manner as those for Soldiers &c.'

The NSR would hardly have got rich on such warrants from Rocester, for most of a prisoner's journey would have been over the Stafford & Uttoxeter from Bromshall Junction, $2\frac{1}{4}$ miles north of Uttoxeter on the main line to Stoke.

By 1879, 13 miles of mostly single track had stretched west through the undulating countryside for twelve years, the blunted thrust by the Great Northern Railway to reach, with running powers, Shrewsbury, by courtesy of the LNWR, and Mid Wales with the cooperation of the Cambrian Railways.

Today, you can walk into the pleasant, airy booking hall at Stafford station and buy a ticket to Paddington, if you have the time and inclination to ignore the Euston main line. Years ago an alternative to Euston meant using a separate booking office at the station, rather remote and small – that of Stafford GNR.

Getting from Stafford to King's Cross via that company was a journey once made by that inveterate traveller, T. R. Perkins, who, by 1932, had travelled every British line carrying regular passenger services. How much was over main line; what proportion over branches? Comparative figures of today would be very different.

Perkins (Thomas Richard) recalled the journey in the *Railway Magazine* in February 1939. He caught the 6.25am to Uttoxeter from Stafford:

The time for departure had nearly arrived before the booking clerk appeared; evidently passengers by that train were not usually many. My request for a ticket to King's Cross occasioned surprise and a little delay, but eventually I obtained it, and was hurried into the now overdue train, which started almost before I had taken my seat.

Not that progress was rapid, for the 6.25am stopped at all stations to collect milk which, even from the Stafford Common area, reached London doorsteps via King's Cross.

World War I put an end to separate staffing at Stafford – the Great Northern's most westerly outpost – and the LNWR took over handling branch trains.

The branch had another fan, a friend of mine, the Rev Noel Benham, whose prep school, Yarlet, overlooked the Stone–Colwich line. In his eighties, he wrote from New Zealand, where he has lived for many years, to recall:

> I remember going on cycle trips from Stone and being pleased to see the Great Northern train at Salt on its way between Stafford and Derby, an interesting little station where one worked the signal oneself if you wanted the train to stop!

World War II gave the ailing branch a lifeline because of the establishment of No. 16 Maintenance Unit, RAF, east of Stafford Common. Afterwards, as overseas bases closed, equipment was returned to the unit for disposal, much of it being handled by rail. The line closed in March 1951, with the exception of the 1¾ miles between the West Coast main line and Stafford Common, which survived for almost a quarter of a century longer.

The track was not lifted for some years, being retained for possible use in mining an extensive field of coal.

Pleasure Excursions

To resorts on or adjacent to the L. & N. W. Railway.

Parties of 50 First Class or 100 Second or Third Class Passengers, when travelling distances not less than 30 miles each way, will be charged **Single Fares** for the double journey.

The tickets will be available for return the **same day only**, and parties can only proceed and return by the trains which stop at the stations where they wish to join and leave the railway.

To obtain the reduced fare tickets application must be made not less than **three days** before the date of the excursion to the District Superintendent, Mr. L. W. HORNE, New Street Station, Birmingham; Mr. ROBBINS, L. & N. W. Agent, or Mr. FORD, Booking Offices, New Street Station; the Parcels Receiving Offices at Birmingham, Dudley, Derby, Coventry, Leamington; or to the L. & N. W. Railway Station Masters.

The following particulars are required :—

1. The exact object of the journey ;
2. The date of the proposed excursion ;
3. The class of carriage and probable number of passengers ;
4. The stations from and trains by which the party will go and return.

These tickets will not be issued to or from London, from or to any place distant more than 30 miles from London ; except that for school parties and parties of 50 first class or 100 second or third class passengers, they will be issued to and from London and any place, irrespective of distance.

Pleasure Party Tickets will not be issued to commercial towns, nor for business purposes. The minimum fare is 1/-. Fractions of a penny will be added in all cases.

Special arrangements can be made for large school parties, irrespective of distance.

The power of refusing to grant any application is reserved.

Crystal Palace, Sydenham.

Pleasure and School Parties can be arranged from stations on the L. & N. W. Railway to the Crystal Palace at low fares including admission. Particulars can be ascertained on application to the Superintendent of the Line, Euston Station, London. Parties are conveyed via Willesden and Kensington to the London, Brighton and South Coast Railway Company's Crystal Palace Station.

Euston Station, London,
July, 1908.

FREDERICK HARRISON, General Manager.

McCorquodale & Co. Limited, Printers, London—Works. Newton. 506

Edwardian summer Awaydays, July 1908. With a fare structure more complicated than today... 'Pleasure Party Tickets will not be issued to commercial towns...'

Gazetteer

CHAPTER 2—BIRMINGHAM: GWR

BIRMINGHAM (SNOW HILL)–WOLVERHAMPTON (LOW LEVEL)
12½ miles
For Priestfield Junction–Cannock Road Junction see also Wolverhampton, Chapter 4.

A dozen miles of challenge and constant change that promise to keep planners busy for years. Some sections are still in rail use, another has been retained for a second Birmingham Cross-City Line. A little of the trackbed is scheduled for industrial development. Part has been adapted for recreation, notably the West Bromwich Parkway, where planners have put pockets of green and pleasant land into a predominantly industrial landscape.

ACTS: 4 August 1845: Oxford Worcester & Wolverhampton Railway; 3 August 1846: Birmingham Wolverhampton & Dudley.

OPENED: April 1854: OW & W: Priestfield–Cannock Road Junction (*Gds*); mixed gauge. 1 July: *Pass*. 14 November 1854: BW & D: Birmingham GWR station (later Snow Hill)–Priestfield Junction; mixed gauge. 25 December 1931:

GWR: The Hawthorns station. 4 August 1966: BR: Smethwick West–Galton Junction; new connection.

CLOSED: 6 March 1972: Birmingham (Snow Hill)–Wolverhampton (Low Level) (*Pass*); Birmingham (Snow Hill)–Langley Green (*Pass*); Birmingham (Snow Hill)–Handsworth & Smethwick (Queen's Head Sidings) (*Gds*); Handsworth Junction–Swan Village North (*Gds*). 12 December 1981: Wednesbury Central–Swan Village CCD. 7 May 1983: Wednesbury Central–Wolverhampton Steel Terminal (Walsall Street). Terminal remains served via Stour Valley.

REMAINS: *Hockley*: platform, Icknield Street (058881); *Handsworth & Smethwick*: platforms, Booth Street (033893); *Wednesbury Central*: platforms, Great Western Street (982945); *Bilston Central*: platforms, Railway Drive (951962); *Priestfield*: platforms, Ward Street (935969).

USES: Trackbed retained throughout. *Birmingham (Snow Hill)*: comprehensive redevelopment. *Soho & Winson Green*: redevelopment of goods yard as a 7 acre business park begun by West Midlands County Council and a private development company, as a partnership, in July 1984 (044888); *Handsworth & Smethwick*: Birmingham Railway Carriage & Wagon Company's works incorporated into Middlemore Industrial Estate (031895); *Handsworth Junction–Swan Village*: from Halford's Lane (022898) to Swan Village reclaimed by WMCC as linear open space called West Bromwich Parkway. It passes beside Kendrick Park, West Bromwich, immediately north of M5 viaduct (016900); *West Bromwich*: platform edges incorporated into landscaped recreation area beside ringway and Queen Square Shopping Centre (004910); *Swan Village*: platforms of BW & D in-filled and incorporated into parkway, which, in 1983, ended at Swan Lane level-crossing (993922); *Swan Village–Wednesbury (Potters Lane)*: WMCC and BR discussing trackbed acquisition for extension of parkway; *Wolverhampton (Low Level)*: main building used as Area Manager's offices.

SWAN VILLAGE–GREAT BRIDGE (HORSELEY FIELDS JUNCTION)
1½ miles
Great Western Railway

Provided a direct link between Birmingham (Snow Hill) and Dudley.

ACT: 3 August 1846: Birmingham Wolverhampton & Dudley.
OPENED: 1 September 1866.
CLOSED: 15 June 1964: *Pass*. 6 October 1967: Swan Village Basin–Horseley Fields Junction. 5 December 1967: Swan Village Junction–Swan Village Basin. 1 January 1968: official date for closure of branch.
USES: *Swan Village*: junction site incorporated into walkway, single-storey factories built on branch trackbed under shadow of gas-holders.

DUDDESTON VIADUCT
½ mile

There are few more striking memorials to railways that were built but never opened. Duddeston viaduct can be viewed comfortably from the windows of trains that pass both ends.

ACT: 3 August 1846.
REMAINS: Entire length, punctuated by demolished arches and embankment stretches removed for factory extensions. Stretches from Birmingham & Oxford at Bordesley, ⅔ mile south of Moor Street (082862) via Upper Trinity Street, across Adderley Street, Allcock Street, Liverpool Street and Great Barr Street to pass north of Montague Street, near Birmingham city centre.

HENLEY-IN-ARDEN–LAPWORTH(ROWINGTON JUNCTION) 3¼ miles
Great Western Railway

A branch that has been closed for a far longer period of time than it was open.

ACT: 23 June 1884: Henley-in-Arden & Birmingham Railway. 1 July 1900: local company taken over by GWR.

OPENED: 6 June 1894: Rowington Junction–Henley-in-Arden terminus (*Pass*). 2 July: *Gds*. 1 July 1898: branch extended to Birmingham & North Warwickshire Railway at Henley-in-Arden. Terminus became a goods station.

CLOSED: 1 January 1915: *Pass*. 1 January 1917: *Gds*. Goods station – B & NW retained. 31 December 1962: Henley-in-Arden goods station, and connection.

REMAINS: Many earthworks. *Henley-in-Arden*: trackbed curves east from B & NW. Abutment beside A34 at north end of main street (154665). Shunt-back into goods station (demolished 1968) was at 154667. Branch crossed Stratford-upon-Avon Canal (once GWR owned) at 188682. *Rowington Junction*: trackbed curves south-west from Birmingham & Oxford main line (193688).

USES: *Lowsonford*: bungalow on trackbed.

CHAPTER 3—BIRMINGHAM: LNWR

HARBORNE JUNCTION–HARBORNE   2½ miles
London & North Western Railway

Provided a classic story of a commuter branch too close to a city's heart to fight road transport once it became established.

ACT: 28 June 1866.
OPENED: 10 August 1874.
CLOSED: 26 November 1934: *Pass*. 4 November 1963: *Gds*.
REMAINS: Abutments of bridge over Birmingham Canal Navigation and short tunnel (bricked up, with single door) under Northbrook Street. Clearly visible from Stour Valley Line (048875).
USES: Trackbed converted into attractive walkway by Birmingham City planning department. *Harborne*: flats on station site (034845).

Intermediate stations were at Icknield Port Road (045873); Rotten Park Road (039869); Hagley Road (032862).

BIRMINGHAM: CURZON STREET STATION
London & North Western Railway

A stout memorial to the Railway Age, ennobled by restoration.

ACT: 6 May 1833.
OPENED: 24 June 1838: London & Birmingham Railway. January 1839: Grand Junction Railway.
CLOSED: 1 July 1854: *Regular pass.* 22 March 1893: *Excursion traffic.* 23 September 1968: *Gds office use.*

BIRMINGHAM: ASTON WINDSOR STREET GOODS   75 chains
London & North Western Railway

Few branches were better revenue earners than this, especially considering its short length.

ACT: 22 July 1878.
OPENED: 1 March 1880.
CLOSED: 12 May 1980.
REMAINS: Trackbed.
USES: Earmarked on closure for industry and warehousing.

BIRMINGHAM: SOHO POOL   56 chains
London & North Western Railway

Smaller than Windsor Street, the branch was useful and busy for many years.

ACT: 16 July 1883.
OPENED: 1 April 1889.
CLOSED: 6 May 1974: *Regular gds.* 1982: Texaco oil terminal.
REMAINS: Trackbed. *Factory Road*: overbridge at northern end of small yard.

CHAPTER 4—WOLVERHAMPTON

Warning If you go by train for a rail walkabout in the town, travel light. There is no left luggage office at the station, busy though it may be.

PRIESTFIELD JUNCTION–CANNOCK ROAD JUNCTION   2 miles
Great Western Railway

ACT: 4 August 1845: Oxford Worcester & Wolverhampton Railway.

OPENED: April 1854: *Gds.* 1 July: *Pass.* Mixed gauge until 1869.

CLOSED: 4 March 1968: Wolverhampton (Low Level)–Cannock Road Junction completely, except shunting neck at north end. Last booked train ran 27 July 1969. 6 March 1972: Birmingham (Snow Hill)–Wolverhampton (Low Level) (*Pass*). 23 May 1973: Priestfield–Wolverhampton (Low Level South) taken out of use. 1982: Wolverhampton (Low Level) closed as parcels concentration depot. BR weekly Traffic Notice of 27 October 1984 stated 'track secured out of use pending removal'.

REMAINS: *Priestfield Junction*: see Chapter 2. *Wolverhampton*: single-bore tunnels under Lower Walsall Street (926985). *Low Level*: station building as incorporated into PCD. To the north: lattice footbridge Lock Street.

USES: *Wolverhampton*: trackbed north of Cannock Road occupied by vehicle scrap yard. Stafford Road works and shed replaced by two industrial estates on A449 (002915). *Cannock Road Junction*: steel bridge which carried lines to Stafford Road shed over Birmingham Canal main line includes a bow girder which separated the two tracks. Lies beside Wolverhampton Junction Railway alongside western end of 1983 spur (918002). *Dunstall Park*: platform edges on Wolverhampton Junction Railway. Station, only one on WJR, closed 4 March 1968 when Shrewsbury trains switched to Wolverhampton (High Level). Stafford Road locomotive shed closed September 1963. Locomotive works, 1 June 1964: official date. Oxley GWR locomotive shed closed March 1967. Site utilised by modern carriage servicing depot.

WOLVERHAMPTON HIGH LEVEL (NORTH JUNCTION)–VICTORIA
BASIN   ½ mile

ACT: 3 August 1846: Shrewsbury & Birmingham Railway.
Branch included in Act of Incorporation.
OPENED: 12 November 1849.
CLOSED: 6 March 1967.
USES: Large warehouse used by builders' merchants, was
part of Herbert Street goods station. Warehouse built 1935
on site of 1858 structure.

WOLVERHAMPTON: LONDON & NORTH WESTERN RAILWAY

REMAINS: *Town centre*: Horseley Fields: two-storey unprepossessing carriage entrance to original LNWR station.
Often mistaken for entrance building. Still awaiting restoration. Future uncertain. *Bushbury*: industrial estate on site
of Bushbury locomotive shed, closed 12 April 1965
(916015). *Wednesfield Heath*: original Grand Junction station
for Wolverhampton was on north side of A460 Cannock
Road (925999); closed 1 January 1873 (*Pass*), 4 October
1965 (*Gds*); demolished.

OXLEY JUNCTION–KINGSWINFORD JUNCTION   12½ miles
Great Western Railway

Unless it is likely to rain, save the branch to the last part of an
itinerary because it is a place where it is pleasant to get away
from town and industry and relax.

ACTS: 4 August 1845: OW & W (Incorporation) Kingswin-
ford Junction–Bromley Basin (1½ miles). 11 July 1905:
GWR: Wolverhampton (Oxley Junction)–Kingswinford.
OPENED: 14 November 1858: Kingswinford Junction–
Bromley Basin. 11 January 1925: Kingswinford branch
(*Gds*). 11 May: Kingswinford branch (*Pass*).
CLOSED: 31 October 1932: *regular pass*. 1 March 1965: Oxley
Junction–Baggeridge Junction (completely).

REMAINS: *Aldersley*: bridges carrying Oxley East and West spurs. *Tettenhall*: station waiting-room building on down side restored by Wolverhampton Borough Council, autumn 1984. Building on never used up platform derelict. Booking office and goods depot used by roofing contractor. Girder bridge over Staffordshire & Worcestershire Canal to south of station (893999). *Compton Halt*: platform (884987). *Penn Halt*: platform (864963).

USES: *Wolverhampton (Oxley Branch Junction)–Castlecroft*: designed by Wolverhampton Borough Council as linear park, named Valley Park 3 December 1974. Joins Kingswinford Branch Railway Walk, developed by South Staffordshire District Council continuing 5½ miles south to Wall Heath. *Wombourn*: station adapted as information centre (870939). *Pensnett Coal Depot–Kingswinford Junction*: still in use. Pensnett signal-box removed to Bridgnorth station, Severn Valley Railway.

CHAPTER 5—BLACK COUNTRY: GWR

WOLVERHAMPTON (PRIESTFIELD JUNCTION)–DUDLEY   4¼ miles
Oxford Worcester & Wolverhampton Railway

Heaviest traffic originating and most industrialised section of the OW & W, but could not compete against more direct LNWR route to London. Local passenger service, Wolverhampton–Dudley–Stourbridge Junction, was totally different in character to the rural one between Stourbridge and Oxford. For a railway born amid many traumas and much bitterness, it has proved remarkably durable – except in the West Midlands.

ACT: 4 August 1845.
OPENED: 1 December 1853: Dudley–Tipton; Tipton Curve (*Gds*). April 1854: Tipton–Priestfield (*Gds*), narrow gauge; 1 July: *Pass*. 1 October 1861: Tipton (*Pass*).

CLOSED: 30 July 1962: Wolverhampton (Low Level)–
Dudley–Stourbridge Junction (*Pass*). 1 January 1968:
Priestfield Junction–Dudley North Junction (*Gds*) (Dudley:
short section retained as Freightliner terminal shunt-back).

REMAINS: *Priestfield Junction*: *see* Birmingham Wolverhampton & Dudley. *Bilston West*: grassed-over platform of station
on embankment beside abutments flanking Coseley Road
(945960). *Princes End & Coseley*: station site in cutting between Bradleys Lane and Fountain Lane. Trackbed continued towards wagon works. Bridge abutments beside
canal by industrial estate (*see* Uses). High bridge over
Birmingham–Wolverhampton dual carriageway (A4123)
(945918). Dudley FLT shunt-back a short distance beyond.
Dudley: Substantial station between Castle Hill and Tipton
Road demolished 1966–7. Lies amid unused railway land.

USES: West Midlands County Council and Wolverhampton,
Sandwell and Dudley Councils have developed Priestfield
Junction–Bilston–Tipton as linear open space, often
linked to adjoining reclaimed derelict land. Features include *Bilston*, where Millfields Road (A4039) has in-filled
overbridge and cutting banked to road level (943963). Footpath curves through cutting to north and Priestfield (1
mile). Associated work at *Daisy Bank & Bradley* and
trackbed course can be traced from humpback bridge in
Highfields Road (948954). Station was demolished, but
another humpback overbridge in Brierley Lane (951947)
was retained as a feature amid reclaimed trackbed and
derelict area. At *Princes End & Coseley*, derelict track can be
viewed from pleasant lattice constructed pedestrian bridge
between Fountain Lane and Bloomfield Road, near the
South Staffordshire Wagon Works, *Tipton*, where part of the
OW & W trackbed has been incorporated into the works
layout, reached from the Stour Valley line. Tipton Canal
Basin branch, served only from the OW & W, was obliterated by an industrial estate, developed 1981–2, together
with the course of the Tipton curve between the OW & W
and the Stour Valley line closed in the 1860s (947927).

Dudley: substantial station demolished to make way for Freightliner terminal, opened 6 November 1967.

STOURBRIDGE TOWN–STOURBRIDGE BASIN GOODS BRANCH

½ mile

Great Western Railway

Curved, partly on 1 in 27 gradient – meant operating problems.

ACTS: 23 July 1858: Oxford Worcester & Wolverhampton: Stourbridge Incline from main line. 30 June 1874: GWR: standard-gauge branch.
OPENED: 1 January 1880: Stourbridge Town–Basin.
CLOSED: c1878: Incline. 20 September 1965: Stourbridge Town–Basin.
REMAINS: *Stourbridge Town*: abutment beside Birmingham Street (A458) widened to dual carriageway, absorbing trackbed at right angles just east of new bus station. Abutments of railway bridge over river Stour in valley below (903844). *Stourbridge Basin*: canal tranship shed.
USES: Stourbridge industrial estate has obliterated site of line. Garage built on site of High Street level-crossing over (A491) road to Wolverhampton.

CORNGREAVES GOODS BRANCH   250yd
Great Western Railway

'Parent' of Old Hill goods branch.

ACT: 14 June 1860: Stourbridge Railway.
OPENED: 1 April 1863.
CLOSED: 12 April 1965.
REMAINS: '... mainly a desolate landscape of scrub woodland, weeds, rosebay willowherb, ald, willow and waste ground, interspersed by derelict buildings, a brickworks ... no railway evidence' (Geoffrey Bannister, October 1984).
USES: Corngreaves industrial estate. Several units built by late 1984.

JUNCTION AND TERMINUS: *Plate 24 (above)* a single-coach branch train waits to leave the junction of Whitacre for Hampton, while an eastbound train for Derby or Nuneaton is in a main line platform. 1902; *Plate 25 (below)* Ashbourne, North Staffordshire Railway terminus on a horse and cattle fair day when livestock special trains were run.

BIDDULPH VALLEY: *Plate 26 (above)* sand from Biddulph to Stoke heads south through Ford Green, 1 May 1967, after the branch had been singled. The left hand track is severed in the distance; *Plate 27 (below)* the scene at Easter 1981, trackbed reclamation in progress. The signal box was later moved to Dilhorne Park station on the Foxfield Railway.

OLD HILL (SPINNERS END) GOODS BRANCH   55 chains
Great Western Railway

Edwardian, short, once tremendously busy.

ACT: 15 August 1904.
OPENED: 1 August 1907.
CLOSED: 10 August 1964.
REMAINS: *Old Hill*: stone setts between former tracks (now reduced to compacted ballast) in goods yard in Upper High Street.
USES: Spinners End industrial estate (West Midlands County Council, 18 mini-units) uses part of site. A roofing centre occupies terminus site in Upper High Street, using yard for storage. Blue brick building, loading bay platform and retaining wall are here. Between terminus and Stourbridge line, part of trackbed used as unofficial footpath to council estate.

LYE HAYES LANE GOODS BRANCH $\frac{3}{4}$ mile
Great Western Railway

Connected to Lye goods yard.

ACT: 14 June 1860: Stourbridge Railway.
OPENED: June 1863.
CLOSED: 10 August 1964.
REMAINS: Lye goods depot (behind Fast Fuel Distributors' depot).
USES: Branch obliterated by Hayes trading estate (light industrial premises), Folkes Road.

OLDBURY & LANGLEY GREEN–OLDBURY   1½ miles
Great Western Railway

A third of this branch survives, serving Albright & Wilson chemical works. Branch notable for the short-lived nature of its passenger service: only thirty years.

ACTS: 21 July 1873: Dudley & Oldbury Junction Railway. 11 August 1881: Name changed to Oldbury Railway. 1 July 1894: Amalgamated with GWR.

OPENED: 7 November 1884: *Gds*. 1 May 1885: *Pass*.

CLOSED: 3 March 1915: *Pass*. 7 September 1964: Oldbury goods depot closed.

REMAINS: *Langley Green*: sharply curved branch platform, through which mineral trains still pass. Oldbury station was between canal and Halesowen Street, which the branch bridged. (989892).

DUDLEY (BLOWERS GREEN JUNCTION)—OLD HILL   2½ miles
Great Western Railway

An intensely worked passenger and freight branch serving an area of high population and industrial concentration.

ACT: 17 July 1862: West Midland Railway: Dudley (Netherton)—Old Hill—Halesowen. Branches: Withymoor and Halesowen: canal basins.

OPENED: 1 March 1878: Dudley–Halesowen. 10 March 1879: Withymoor Basin branch (67 chains).

CLOSED: 15 June 1964: Dudley–Old Hill (*Pass*). 5 July 1965: Withymoor Basin branch (renamed Netherton 1 August 1921). 1 January 1968: Dudley–Old Hill (*Gds*).

REMAINS: *Blowers Green*: station closed 30 July 1962 (*Pass*). Booking hall at street level in Netherton New Road, in private use. Platform remains on OW & W in cutting below, short distance from southern mouth of Dudley tunnel. Site of Blowers Green Junction (with Old Hill branch) visible. Overbridge in Netherton New Road at 943894 is excellent viewpoint to trace trackbed towards Baptist End (938887). Trackbed tapered and grassed at site of Baptist End Halt. *Windmill End*: railway bridge abutments at Windmill End Canal Junction (954883). *Old Hill*: Wright's Lane: brick abutment (with GR pillar-box) by cleared site of High Street Halt. Station Road: substantial abutments of branch overbridge, just short of South Junction, which was at end of

Birmingham platform and in the middle of the down platform used by Stourbridge trains.

USES: *Blowers Green*: Overbridge blocked off, yard developed on trackbed alongside former junction. *Baptist End*: St Peter's Rd: pleasant, grassed walkway (947887). *Netherton goods branch*: large water tank from north side of Northfield Road level-crossing (948878) is in active retirement at Eardington on the Severn Valley Railway.

OLD HILL–HALESOWEN   1½ miles
Great Western Railway

ACTS: 17 July 1862: West Midland Railway: Dudley–Halesowen. 2 August 1898: Halesowen–Halesowen Basin.

OPENED: 1 March 1878: *Pass*. 2 April 1902: Halesowen Basin branch (1 mile).

CLOSED: 5 December 1927: *Pass*. 9 September 1968: Halesowen goods depot. 1 October 1969: Old Hill–Halesowen Basin.

REMAINS: *Old Hill*: Trackbed curved away sharply from Stourbridge line to reach Haden tunnel (151yd) under high, wooded ridge surmounted by houses. Trackbed continues parallel to main road to Halesowen, on low embankment among trees. *Coombes*: substantial abutment on north side of Coombes Road (967847).

USES: *Old Hill*: timber yard on site of goods yard and branch trackbed. *Coombes*: car park of modern Makro store on high embankment built over trackbed. *Halesowen*: station site redeveloped as industrial estate off Mucklow Hill–A456 Halesowen bypass.

HALESOWEN–NORTHFIELD (HALESOWEN JUNCTION)   6 miles
Great Western & Midland Joint

'The most spectacular abandoned track in the West Midlands' (*Birmingham Evening Mail* 'Out Walking' writer, Geoff Allen).

ACTS: 17 July 1862: West Midland Railway: Halesowen

Branch and Halesowen Basin branch. 5 July 1865: Halesowen & Bromsgrove Branch Railway. 13 July 1876: name changed to Halesowen Railway. 1 August 1870: Bromsgrove section abandoned. 29 July 1906: Halesowen Railway vested in GW/MR jointly (back-dated 30 June).

OPENED: 10 September 1883: Halesowen–Northfield.

CLOSED: April 1919: *Regular pass.* 1 September 1958: Old Hill–Longbridge (workmen's service). 4 January 1960: Longbridge – Halesowen Junction – Birmingham (New Street) (workmen's service). 6 January 1964: Halesowen–Rubery (completely). 6 July 1964: Rubery–Longbridge West (completely).

REMAINS: *Halesowen*: abutment and embankments flanking minor road (974823). *Frankley*: trackbed emerges from Round Saw Croft wood just north of M5 (977794), and runs downhill towards Hunnington. *Longbridge*: three-arch bridge on trackbed walkway.

USES: *Halesowen*: trackbed severed by dual carriageway of A456. *Hunnington*: station converted to private house (967813). *Frankley*: trackbed and cutting in-filled immediately south of M5 (981790). Motorway also severed trackbed at right angles. Trackbed converted into walkway incorporated into new housing estate. *Longbridge*: another three-arch railway overbridge incorporated into landscaped area in Boleyn Road, which crosses trackbed walkway on new bridge (985785). Walkway links estate with Holly Hill shopping centre.

CHAPTER 6—BLACK COUNTRY: LNWR

DUDLEY–SEDGELEY JUNCTION–DUDLEY PORT JUNCTION (HIGH LEVEL) 1¼ miles

London & North Western Railway

Once used by one of the most intensively worked pull-and-push services in the Region.

ACTS: 3 August 1846: South Staffordshire Junction Railway.

24 July 1851: Sedgeley Junction–Dudley Port. 1 March 1850: Dudley–Walsall.

OPENED: 2 January 1854: Sedgeley Junction–Dudley Port.

CLOSED: 6 July 1964: Sedgeley Junction–Dudley Port (High Level) (completely). Dudley–Dudley Port (High Level) (*Pass*). Also: Dudley–Dudley Port (Low Level)–Walsall (*Pass*). An engineer's siding was retained from Dudley Port (High Level) until 5 January 1965.

USES: Entire branch, Sedgeley Junction–Dudley Port (High Level), bulldozed and levelled and developed as Coburn Court private housing estate, opened 1983. *Dudley Port*: Low Level station on South Staffordshire line, was between Stour Valley line overbridge and that of Park Lane East; long demolished.

WEDNESBURY TOWN–JAMES BRIDGE (DARLASTON LOOP)

2½ miles

London & North Western Railway

The branch passenger service was one of the earliest casualties of tramway competition in the West Midlands.

ACT: 23 July 1855: South Staffordshire Railway.

OPENED: 14 September 1863.

CLOSED: 1 November 1887: *Pass*. 24 November 1963: Fallings Heath (Lloyds works sidings)–Darlaston Junction. 1 January 1968: Wednesbury (Patent Shaft sidings)–Fallings Heath crossing. Summer 1980: Wednesbury Town (Exchange Sidings)–Patent Shaft sidings.

REMAINS: *Wednesbury*: trackbed of branch in cutting beside Potter's Lane, running from junction by site of Wednesbury Town station (closed 6 July 1964). *Darlaston*: trackbed curves from junction with Grand Junction route into works.

USES: *Darlaston*: trackbed reclaimed as open space between Darlaston Green and Walsall Road. Darlaston station was in cutting between A461 and A462 roads. It was almost a mile from Darlaston station on the Grand Junction (called James Bridge 1863–89). It closed 18 January 1965.

WEDNESBURY–TIPTON (BLOOMFIELD JUNCTION). PRINCES END
BRANCH   2¾ miles
London & North Western Railway

Branch passenger services were another comparatively early victim of road competition.

ACT: 23 July 1855: South Staffordshire Railway.
OPENED: 14 September 1863.
CLOSED: 1 January 1916: *Pass*. 6 April 1981: *Gds*.
REMAINS: Trackbed easy to trace.
USES: West Midland County Council considered conversion to linear open space.

WALSALL (RYECROFT JUNCTION)–ANGLESEA SIDINGS   5½ miles
London & North Western Railway

An important section of the former South Staffordshire cross-country route.

ACT: 2 July 1847: South Staffordshire Junction Railway.
OPENED: 9 April 1849.
CLOSED: 18 January 1965: *Pass*. 19 March 1984: *Gds*.
REMAINS: *Walsall*: bridge which carried avoiding line over (019001). *Rushall*: bridge under B4154. *Brownhills*: bridges under A452 and A5 (dual carriageway). Level-crossing on minor road (059065).

CHAPTER 7—COVENTRY, RUGBY, LEAMINGTON SPA

COVENTRY: HUMBER ROAD JUNCTION–THREE SPIRES JUNCTION
                                                          3½ miles
London & North Western Railway

Known, on official documents, by two titles: Coventry Avoiding Line and Coventry Loop Line. Goods only. Three enthusiasts' specials were the only passenger trains ever to use it.

ACT: 26 July 1907.

OPENED: 10 August 1914.

CLOSED: 10 November 1963: Humber Road Junction–Gosford Green: 1984 Gosford Green–Three Spires Junction. 26 February 1967: Royal Naval stores depot closed: connection severed.

REMAINS: Trackbed easy to trace using street maps.

USES: *Gosford Green*: small commercial developments on part of goods yard site. *Bell Green Road* (351815) – *Three Spires Junction* (341827): projected road. Birmingham A-Z 1982 showed route from Bell Green Road (B4109) and goods depot (351811) to Three Spires Junction as southern end of proposed Coventry–M6 (Junction 3) link road. Gosford Green yard was at 348788.

RUGBY–LEAMINGTON SPA (AVENUE) $14\frac{1}{4}$ miles
London & North Western Railway

Ten miles of the branch survive to feed the Rugby Cement Works at Southam, trains using a fragment of the Weedon branch after reversal at Marton Junction.

ACTS: 13 August 1846: Rugby & Leamington Railway. 17 November 1846: company purchased by LNWR.

OPENED: 1 March 1851. 27 March 1882: Rugby–Dunchurch doubled.

CLOSED: 15 September 1958: Weedon–Leamington Spa (Avenue) (*Pass*). 15 June 1959: Rugby–Leamington Spa (Avenue) (*Pass*). 4 April 1966: Marton Junction–Leamington Spa (Avenue) (completely).

REMAINS: Branch crossed the Grand Union Canal at 353649. *Leamington*: Industrial estate on trackbed and also site of GWR locomotive shed (327648). Avenue station site and goods yard partly occupied by large car showrooms. Coal concentration depot to north served by trains using route between Avenue and Milverton stations.

BERKSWELL–KENILWORTH JUNCTION   4¼ miles
London & North Western Railway

Berkswell is less than 4 miles from Hampton-in-Arden, its neighbour nearer Birmingham (New Street), and once junction of the Whitacre branch: the Stonebridge Railway. This was one of the earliest railways in the West Midlands. The Coventry Avoiding Line was among the last to be built in the Region.

ACT: 18 July 1881. Also: Kenilworth Junction–Milverton (for Warwick) doubling.
OPENED: 2 March 1884: *Gds*. 2 June: *Pass*.
CLOSED: 18 January 1965: Berkswell–Kenilworth closed (*Pass*). Berkswell & Balsall Common, Kenilworth and Warwick (Milverton): stations closed. 17 January 1969: line closed completely.
REMAINS: *Berkswell*: trackbed fenced off (245776). *Kenilworth Junction*: trackbed leaves Coventry branch in deep, wooded cutting (299731). *Kenilworth*: station, almost a mile south of the junction, was at 292716. Bridge over A46 demolished (297735).
USES: *Kenilworth*: goods yard used by builders' merchant. *See also*: Kenilworth History & Archaeology Society Leaflet no. 5, *Kenilworth Station*, for details of stations, including preserved stonework of original one in 1844.

CHAPTER 8—MIDLAND PRESENCE

WHITACRE–HAMPTON   6 miles
Birmingham & Derby Junction

First line in Britain to lose its main-line status. One of most aged forgotten railways in the West Midlands.

ACT: 19 May 1836: The Stonebridge Railway.
OPENED: 12 August 1839.
CLOSED: 1 January 1917: *Pass*. 24 April 1930: *Regular gds*.

1 May 1939: Whitacre–Maxstoke (*Gds*).

REMAINS: *Maxstoke*: bridge abutment beside River Blythe visible in trees near northbound carriageway of M6 which breaches trackbed (215866). *Stonebridge*: trackbed absorbed by widened A452 (209838). Bridge under A45 carries slip road (205831).

BIRMINGHAM: SUFFOLK STREET GOODS BRANCH   76 chains
Midland Railway

Smaller than the Midland's main Birmingham goods station at Lawley Street, yet right in the city's heart. Ran from Five Ways–Church Road Junction–Suffolk Street, known as Worcester Wharf until 1892.

ACT: 18 July 1881.
OPENED: 1 July 1887.
CLOSED: 6 March 1967.
REMAINS: *Church Road*: low embankment running behind down platform to former junction with Birmingham West Suburban Railway immediately west of station.
USES: *Suffolk Street*: goods yard site of Stanier House.

WOLVERHAMPTON (CRANE STREET JUNCTION)–WALSALL (RYE-CROFT JUNCTION)   6¾ miles
Midland Railway

Like the Whitacre–Hampton line, destined to end its day broken into two dead-end branches.

ACT: 29 June 1865: Wolverhampton & Walsall Railway. 1 July 1875: bought by LNWR. 1 August 1876: sold to Midland Railway.
OPENED: 1 November 1872. 1 July 1879: Wolverhampton & Midland Junction Railway: Walsall (Lichfield Road Junction)–North Walsall Junction.
CLOSED: 5 January 1931: Wolverhampton (High Level)– Walsall via Wednesfield (*Pass*). 28 September 1964: Birchills: line severed for M6 motorway construction

(990998); Short Heath–Birchills power station (completely). 7 December 1964: Willenhall (Stafford Street)–Short Heath. 1 November 1965: Wednesfield–Willenhall (Stafford Street). 1 May 1967: Walsall (Lichfield Road Junction)–North Walsall Junction (official date). 12 May 1980: Birchills power station–Walsall (Ryecroft Junction). March 1981: Wolverhampton (Heath Town Junction)–Wednesfield (Midland) last used. Track still in situ autumn 1984. 1984: Wednesfield Road goods depot (Midland) taken out of use.

REMAINS: *Willenhall*: large station site awaited development 1982 (989962). Weighbridge at entrance in Stafford Street. *Short Heath*: Clark's Lane: station site by modern fire station. Overbridge removed and trackbed tapered (994973). *Pouk Hill*: high abutment on east side of Bloxwich Lane (wide and busy) (998991). *Walsall*: North Walsall Junction site in cutting beside Bloxwich Road (A34) (009999). Station was on opposite (west) side of road. Left-hand fork was Walsall Avoiding Line; right-hand spur to LNWR and station. Facing west: cutting towards Birchills power station. *Coal Pool Lane*: Avoiding line overbridge abutment flanking Rugeley line (015999). Mill Lane: Ryecroft Shed site (018998).

USES: *Willenhall*: linear open space developed on trackbed from Noose Lane (956992) through town centre to reclaimed land immediately west of M6 (985998). Includes Willenhall station site.

ALDRIDGE–BROWNHILLS   4 miles
Midland Railway

The tip of the branch has been incorporated into the Chasewater Light Railway—a splendid living memorial to a once busy mineral line.

ACTS: 13 July 1876. 6 August 1880: extension: Walsall Wood–Norton Canes.

OPENED: 1 April 1882: Aldridge–Brownhills (*Gds*). 1 November 1882: Brownhills–Cannock Chase (*Gds*). 1 July 1884: Aldridge–Brownhills (*Pass*).

CLOSED: 31 March 1930: Aldridge–Brownhills (Watling Street) (*Pass*); latter station completely. By September 1960: Walsall Wood–Brownhills (NCB junction). 3 September 1962: Aldridge–Walsall Wood.

REMAINS: *Aldridge*: branch junction (053055): site overgrown by trees. View it, and site of Aldridge station (closed 18 January 1965) from Station Road on opposite side of Walsall–Castle Bromwich line. Trackbed of Brownhills branch visible to north of junction site. *Walsall Wood*: Coppy Lane: humped overbridge. Sweeping views of trackbed approaching from junction and heading north to Vigo Road (another overbridge). Lichfield Road/Coppice Road: station site. Landscaped, and cutting in-filled almost to road level, but road overbridge retained. Small box-shaped subway incorporates smoke-blackened roof. Heavily vandalised it is a walkway under A461 between two landscaped areas of open land. Nearby: Brookland Road overbridge demolished, road raised and cutting grassed to provide sense of space in built-up area. Succeeds. Coppice Road: humped overbridge. Bridge abutments where branch crossed the Walsall–Lichfield line (041054). Branch crossed canal at 042053. Brownhills station was on north side of A452, and ran under A5 (now dual carriageway) at 037065, continuing north to Chasewater.

USES: *Walsall Wood*: industrial estate on trackbed (047037). *Chasewater*: light railway headquarters (033073).

CHAPTER 9—NORTH STAFFORDSHIRE

ETRURIA–KIDSGROVE. POTTERIES LOOP LINE $6\frac{1}{4}$ miles
North Staffordshire Railway

What would Arnold Bennett think if he tried to find the Loop Line today? 'A country lane in a city', to the Greenway's creators it may be. But so much has changed. Gone are the pit spoilheaps, deep clay-pits and bottle kilns, which Loop passengers once glimpsed out of windows—if they could see far enough through the smoke and grime of the area. A pleasant adapted trackbed now picks its way through a far more attractive scene, though still urban in character.

'The North Staffordshire Railway binds together the range of Pottery towns, like a thread stringing beads'—the view of Measom's LNWR guide, 1861. The Loop had still to be threaded—and to become one of the NSR's money-spinners.

ACTS: 2 July 1847: Etruria–Shelton. 13 August 1859: Shelton–Hanley. 5 July 1865: Hanley–Kidsgrove.

OPENED: 1850: Etruria–Shelton (*Gds*). 20 December 1861: Shelton–Hanley (*Gds*). January 1862: Etruria–Shelton (*Pass*). 13 July 1864: Shelton–Hanley (*Pass*). 1 November 1873: Hanley–Burslem. 1 December 1873: Burslem–Tunstall. 1 October 1874: Tunstall–Goldenhill. 15 November 1875: Goldenhill–Kidsgrove. Temporarily re-opened: Kidsgrove–Goldenhill (Park Farm coal bunker): 1 June 1971.

CLOSED: 4 October 1943: Waterloo Road station (completely) (878482). 2 March 1964: Etruria–Kidsgrove (*Pass*). 3 January 1966: Shelton (Waterloo Road oil depot)–Birchenwood (*Gds*). 4 August 1969: Etruria–Hanley (*Gds*). January 1976: Kidsgrove–Goldenhill (*mineral*).

REMAINS: *Etruria*: junction with Stoke–Macclesfield main line was immediately north of Etruria Road overbridge (865469). *Etruria Junction–Etruria*: trackbed through Shelton steelworks abandoned. *Hanley*: tunnel mouth of original Hanley branch station (880477). *Waterloo Road*: station buildings (878482). *Cobridge*: Furnival Street tunnel in-filled 1967 (876488). *Goldenhill*: station was at 862536. *Goldenhill–Kidsgrove*: 1¾ mile trackbed from site of Park Farm opencast coal site (858539) undeveloped yet. Descends to Kidsgrove in long, shallow cutting between houses to site of sidings beside main line north of Kidsgrove station. Substantial brick abutment beside A50 visible from main line (836548).

USES: The Loopline Greenway stretches from Hanley through Burslem to Tunstall. Well signposted. *Burslem*: Hot Lane bridge reconstructed (876494). Station site is an open space. Smokebox of No. 3817 within sight of A50 (869502). *Tunstall*: station was at 862513. Preserved signal on site. *Pitts Hill*: locomotive driving wheels by station site (865521).

HARECASTLE DIVERSION   2½ miles
British Rail

Conscience need not be troubled by viewing the trackless mouths of the Harecastle tunnels, for the Diversion that has replaced the original NSR route runs through green and pleasant countryside. Banished is a black and smoky stretch of railway.

ACT: Original: North Staffordshire Railway 26 June 1846.
OPENED: 9 October 1848.
CLOSED: 27 June 1966 on opening of Diversion.
REMAINS: Harecastle Middle tunnel. North portal (840536) Harecastle South Tunnel. South portal (848521). Chatterley sidings. Mostly derelict February 1984. (850515)
USES: Harecastle tunnel has been opened out and incorporated into Diversion (838540).

Diversion runs from north (839537) to south (851509).

CHATTERLEY SIDINGS—TALKE-O'-TH'-HILL   2½ miles
Private/North Staffordshire Railway

Served a colliery and industrial area with distinction.

ACT: 28 June 1861.
OPENED: 1860 (ahead of Act).
CLOSED: Tip of branch: 27 April 1931. Remainder: 1955.
REMAINS: Chesterton Junction, some 300yd west of NSR Stoke—Congleton main line, was at 847510.

USES: Trackbed bisected by A500 dual carriageway (846511). Trackbed swallowed by A500/A34 interchange and again bisected just west (828518).

CHATTERLEY SIDINGS—CHESTERTON   1½ miles
North Staffordshire Railway

Pits and iron works provided the staple diet of this mineral-only branch, for which the NSR got a Light Railway Order.

ACT: 29 July 1864.
OPENED: January 1866. 16 October 1964: branch junction realigned from north- to south-facing, continuing to Bradwell sidings.
CLOSED: 21 June 1968.
REMAINS: Rusting track beside down main line. Old Junction was at 851503. Parkhouse colliery, last branch terminus, was beside A34 (836504). Originally, branch continued under A34 and beyond.
USES: Trackbed pierced by A500 (846511).

ALSAGER—SILVERDALE: AUDLEY MINERAL LINE   7½ miles

Another of the intensively worked mineral branches which provided the North Staffordshire Railway with so much of its traffic and revenue.

ACT: 29 July 1864.
OPENED: 24 July 1870: Alsager (East Junction)–Honeywall Junction (*Gds*). 28 June 1880 (*Pass*). 1 October 1880: Honeywall East Curve.
CLOSED: 27 April 1931: Alsager–Keele (*Pass*). 18 June 1962: Audley–Keele (*Gds*); Alsager locomotive shed (LMS 5E). 7 January 1963: Alsager–Audley (*Gds*). Alsager–Diglake NCB opencast site retained to 1966–7. 22 September 1968: Alsager (East Junction)–Alsager Yard (out of use).
REMAINS: Trackbed easily traceable. *Alsager*: Abutments flank suburban road (807551).
USES: Trackbed bisected by A500 dual carriageway (817521).

ALSAGER–SANDBACH   6½ miles
North Staffordshire Railway

After being an early casualty of railway politics—it was just possible the branch could have provided the NSR with a springboard towards Liverpool—it had a quiet existence, surviving into the 1970s because of its ability to take some pressure off Crewe freight routes.

ACT: 26 June 1846.

OPENED: 21 January 1852: Alsager (Lawton Junction)–Ettiley Heath (*Gds*). December 1866: Ettiley Heath–Sandbach (*Gds*). 3 July 1893: Alsager–Sandbach (*Pass*).

CLOSED: 28 July 1930: *Pass*. 4 January 1971: *Gds*.

REMAINS: *Alsager*: Lawton Junction site amid fields east of A5011 (805554). *Lawton*: crossing-house site by B5077 being restored 1983. Overbridge on B5078 (795567). *Wheelock*: booking hall and station house beside A534 in private use. Below, in deep, wooded cutting, brick platform approached by overgrown ramp. Trent & Mersey Canal crossed to east (758593).

USES: *Day Green*: high overbridge across minor road carries trackbed footpath (782578). *Hassell Green*: station house with notable chimneypots close to viaduct carrying M6 across trackbed. Platform remains (775582). Signal-box and crossing gates removed to Hadlow Road, Wirral Country Park. To west of station house, trackbed bulldozed and incorporated into Malkins Bank golf course by Congleton Borough Council. *Sandbach*: Ettiley Heath goods shed and siding area in commercial use. Access via horse landing beside Elworthy Road (B5079) to trackbed walk, which continues north under hump-backed bridge. *Elton Crossing*: keeper's house (738609). Signal-box removed to Cheddleton. Immediately north, approach road to Foden Trucks Works straightened by new road across in-filled cutting (737611). Trackbed walk resumes, curving north towards Sandbach station, a short distance away.

NORTH RODE–UTTOXETER (CHURNET VALLEY)   27¾ miles
North Staffordshire Railway

If you want to remember the atmosphere of the *rural* Knotty, and discover some of Britain's least known beauty spots, this is the area to go. But beware! Leek Brook is still the junction of two busy mineral lines: to Caldon quarry, and to Oakamoor sand sidings, 7¾ miles south.

ACT: 26 June 1846.
OPENED: 13 July 1849.
CLOSED: 7 November 1960: North Rode–Leek (*Pass*: work-men's services continued until complete closure on 15 June 1964). 4 January 1965: Leek–Uttoxeter (*Pass*); Oakamoor–Uttoxeter (*Gds*). 6 July 1970: Leek–Leek Brook Junction (*Gds*).
REMAINS: *North Rode*: viaduct over Macclesfield Canal (908655). *Leek*: station demolished, pub which had door to platform renamed. Bricked-up tunnel immediately north. A53 overbridge at southern end of demolished platforms (979539). *Consall*: station with platforms over Caldon Canal demolished (001489), but railway cottages survive. *Oaka-moor*: tunnel. Trackless (052447).
USES: *Rushton*: signal-box preserved at Dinting Railway Centre. Station offered for sale at £78,000 in September 1984. 'Former Railway Station in stone of interesting design, superbly converted to luxury house, in large garden with platform ... Idyllic situation,' stated the agents. One of only three Churnet Valley stations saved from demo-lition, it lies beside the Staffordshire Way heading south, and the complementary Mow Cop Trail, running north (935625). The Staffordshire Way uses trackbed south to Rudyard Lake (1¾ miles). This was the site of Leek & Mani-fold 10¼in gauge railway 1978–80. The Mow Cop Trail runs north from Rushton for a mile to 931634. From Rushton, trackbed walkable to northern outskirts of Leek (972567) and lane leading to A523. *Leek*: generous station and yard site on west of town being progressively redeveloped

GOODS ONLY, PASSENGER ONLY: *Plate 28 (above)* the goods-only Chesterton branch served the large Parkhouse colliery. 'Jinty' tank No 47664 begins the descent to the main line on 25 June 1964; *Plate 29 (below)* the passenger-only Cold Meece branch carried millions of workers to an ROF factory in the country between Stone and Norton Bridge.

PRE 1923 MEMORIES: *Plate 30 (above)* a Great Northern Railway outpost: the now-demolished Stafford Common, grand enough for a town rather than a scattered rural community; *Plate 31 (below)* Potteries industrial scene about 1925. Pinnox Crossing from the Loop Line, Whitfield locomotive *Edward VII* shunts past Pinnox Crossing Box, now preserved at the Chasewater Light Railway, Brownhills. Pinnox Paddy platform right, beyond crossing.

(979559). Goods shed extant. *Cheddleton*: station restored as headquarters of North Staffordshire Railway Association. BR track from Leek Brook Junction to Oakamoor passes platform. *Alton Towers*: station restored. *Oakamoor*: trackbed incorporated into industrial estate. Trackbed from just south of village (052446) to Denstone (100404), nearly 3 miles, is official walkway. *Rocester*: modern works of J. C. Bamford Excavators in extensive landscaped and laked grounds which have swallowed station site and junction of Ashbourne branch (101392). *Spath*: B5030 was site of Britain's first automatic half-barrier crossing, installed February 1961 (085352). *Uttoxeter*: A50 is now dual carriageway where it crossed trackbed (087347).

ROCESTER–ASHBOURNE   7 miles

An early NSR branch, mainly in Derbyshire, which sprung to life and was doubled when the LNWR opened its branch from Buxton. Henceforth, the fortunes of both branches were intertwined.

ACT: 22 July 1848.
OPENED: 31 May 1852.
CLOSED: 1 November 1954: Uttoxeter–Ashbourne–Buxton (*Pass*). 1 June 1964: *Gds*.
REMAINS: Section of trackbed.
USES: *Rocester*: JCB Excavator works straggle junction. *Norbury & Ellastone*: station in private use, garden utilises trackbed. *Clifton*: station and goods yard used as coal depot. Crossing box removed to NSR Cheddleton. Houses on trackbed. *Ashbourne*: swimming pool on station site. Goods shed in commercial use. Goods yard now a lorry park.

BIDDULPH VALLEY: STOKE–MILTON JUNCTION–CONGLETON
                                                    12½ miles

Strolling the pastoral trackbed at the northern end of the valley between Biddulph and Congleton, it is easy to forget how it was once ravaged by pits and iron works and spoil tips. Chatterley Whitfield Mining Museum encapsulates the spirit of the valley far better than the trackbed ever can.

ACT: 24 July 1854.

OPENED: 3 August 1859: Stoke (Stoke Junction)–Congleton (Brunswick Wharf) (*Gds*). 1 June 1864: (*Pass*). Formal date.

CLOSED: 11 July 1927 (*Pass*). 1 December 1963: Congleton Upper and Lower Junctions–Congleton (Brunswick Wharf). 1 April 1968: Biddulph (Victoria Colliery)–Congleton Lower Junction. 14 July 1976: Ford Green–Victoria Colliery. 4 March 1979: Milton Junction–Ford Green.

REMAINS: *Ford Green*: Trackbed flanking B5051. *Brindley Ford*: trackbed flanking demolished bridge over Bull Lane (878568). *Mossley*: A527 bridge abutments. Embankment alongside (885612). *Congleton*: trackbed of Brunswick Wharf section beneath electrified main line. Also spur Lower–Upper Junctions. (879629)

USES: *Ford Green*: Stoke-on-Trent City Council bought tall signal-box which controlled crossing of B5051 for £5 (888508). It is now the property of the Foxfield Light Railway and installed at Dilhorne Park station.

LONGTON ADDERLEY GREEN & BUCKNALL RAILWAY   3½ miles

A short, tremendously busy, little known mineral line at the heart of the Potteries.

ACTS: 16 July 1866: Longton Adderley Green & Bucknall Railway. 14 May 1895: NSR takeover from 1 January. Abandonment of approx ¼ mile authorised.

OPENED: 24 September 1875.

CLOSED: 23 December 1963: Millfield Junction–Park Hall colliery. 6 July 1964: Botteslow Junction–Adderley Green.

REMAINS: Several road bridges.

USES: *Normacot*: trackbed from Millfield Junction lay in cutting — in-filled (923432). Levelled to Anchor Road (919447). Walkway north to Fenton Road Bucknall (900470).

STOKE–MARKET DRAYTON   16¾ miles

The NSR would have been content to go no further than collieries around Apedale on the rural western outskirts of the Potteries, but it was forced into a foray into the thinly populated Shropshire countryside simply to keep out the Great Western.

ACTS: 26 June 1846: Stoke–Newcastle-under-Lyme. 13 August 1859: Silverdale & Newcastle Railway private railway made public. 29 July 1864: Silverdale–Market Drayton.

OPENED: 6 September 1852: Stoke–Newcastle (*Gds*). February 1862: Newcastle–Silverdale (*Gds*). 7 April 1862: Newcastle–Silverdale (*Pass*). 1 February 1870: Silverdale–Market Drayton.

CLOSED: 7 May 1956: Silverdale–Market Drayton (*Pass*). 2 March 1964: Stoke–Silverdale (*Pass*). 8 August 1966: Newcastle–Brampton Siding (*Gds*). 19 May 1967: Silverdale–Market Drayton closed for through freight traffic and completely except Brampton–Madeley Chord. 14 February 1966: Stoke (Newcastle Junction)–Brampton Siding (*Gds*).

REMAINS: *Stoke*: trackbed curves and climbs away from the main line towards Newcastle ridge, on low embankment beside locomotive stable sidings. Trackbed severed by A500 at 871461. *Newcastle*: two tunnels under Shelton New Road (145 and 577yd) in-filled with pit waste (855462). Station was at 852643. *Madeley Road*: station site (774422).

USES: *Newcastle*: station yard in industrial use. *Norton-in-Hales*: station house in private use (700390). *Pipe Gate*: railway overbridge demolished and A51 improved (727408). *Market Drayton*: station site in industrial use (672348). A53 bypass across trackbed (672351). Houses built on trackbed at Brownhills (676358).

TRENTHAM–TRENTHAM PARK   1¼ miles

Even though Trentham Gardens were within sight of, and
within easy walking distance of, Trentham main line station,
the NSR felt it worth while to build the branch from a junction
facing north towards Stoke. Worthy of memory as a piece of
Edwardian initiative that paid off.

ACT: 21 August 1907.
OPENED: 1 April 1910.
CLOSED: 1 May 1913: Hanford Road Halt. 11 September
    1939: *Regular pass.* 1 October 1957: excursion traffic ceased
    and freight-less line closed completely.
REMAINS: Trent & Mersey Canal bridged at 880412. Tren-
    tham Park station was at 869413. Extension bridge across
    A34 (now dual carriageway) was at 867412.

COLD MEECE BRANCH   1½ miles

This was a passenger branch. Freight traffic of Swynnerton
Royal Ordnance Factory was handled, together with some
passengers, at Badnall Wharf on the Crewe–Stafford main
line, immediately west. Nothing evocative remains to be seen
of the wartime branch.

OPENED: 5 August 1941 (officially).
CLOSED: 28 June 1958.
REMAINS: Swynnerton Junction. Site at 875325. Low bridge
    abutments at 860322.
USES: *Cold Meece*: government buildings on station site
    (856325). Factory lay to north towards Swynnerton Park
    and Village.

THE LEEK & MANIFOLD LIGHT RAILWAY   8½ miles

'On the whole, there is little to regret in the advent of the railway. From the utilitarian standpoint it has placed a once very
remote pastoral district within reach of a market for its milk,
and even the most conservative lover of nature undefiled is

bound to admit that the making of the line has done wonderfully little to desecrate the scenery'—Charles Mansfield, Staffordshire, 1910.

ACT: 6 March 1899.
OPENED: 27 June 1904.
CLOSED: 12 March 1934.
REMAINS: Every remain can, happily, be classed under 'Uses'.
USES: *Waterhouses*: 'Manifold Track' starts in middle of village on A523. Signposted, surfaced, fenced, you cannot stray— or ignore the Redhurst–Butterton road stretch. *Hulme End*: station site is road depot. Incorporates locomotive shed. The Light Railway Hotel, one of three which the NSR owned, was renamed the Manifold Valley Hotel in May 1984 by new owners.

WATERHOUSES BRANCH   1 mile

Hardly surprisingly, the village of Waterhouses was no more able to support a passenger or goods service than the Light Railway, and even in wartime, the LMS felt it could handle local traffic from elsewhere.

ACT: None. Light Railway Order of 6 March 1899 was adequate for the whole line from Leek Brook Junction.
OPENED: 1 July 1905.
CLOSED: 30 September 1935: Leek–Waterhouses passenger service withdrawn. 1 March 1943: Caldon Junction–Waterhouses completely.
REMAINS: *Waterhouses*: NSR goods shed. That of L & M demolished. Steps up to station platform.

BURTON UPON TRENT–TUTBURY   5¼ miles

A short branch which took the North Staffordshire Railway to the busiest fringe town that it served.

ACTS: 26 June 1846. 13 July 1863: Stretton Junction–Hawkins

Lane Junction. 25 July 1872: Great Northern Railway. Act included Egginton–Dove Junction.

OPENED: 11 September 1848: Burton–Marston Junction. 1 April 1868: Stretton–Hawkins Lane Junction. January 1878: Egginton–Dove Junction (GNR) (*Gds*). 1 April 1878: Egginton–Dove Junction (*Pass*).

CLOSED: 1 January 1949: Burton–Tutbury intermediate stations closed. 13 June 1960: passenger service withdrawn. 4 April 1966: Horninglow–North Stafford Junction (½ mile). 30 January 1967: Horninglow–Stretton Junction. 6 May 1968: Stretton–Egginton Junction; Dove Junction–Marston Junction; Burton (NSR)–Stretton Junction. July 1968: Stretton–Hawkins Lane Junction.

USES: Horninglow: cafe, easily recognised as former station (251263). Horninglow–Stretton (1 mile) – trackbed converted into road, opened 1 September 1983.

STAFFORD–BROMSHALL JUNCTION–UTTOXETER   15 miles

An unsolved mystery of North Staffordshire Railway history is why the company placed Great Northern services on the title page (which included directors' names) of its 'Time Tables' for some years. Stafford and Uttoxeter trains, linked to those on the NSR Tutbury–Burton, and Ashbourne branches, were included in the table. But there was a sting in the tale of small print: 'The Trains on this page do not run in connection with other Main or Branch Line Trains.'

ACT: 29 July 1862: Great Northern Railway.

OPENED: 23 December 1867; Stafford–Bromshall Junction.

CLOSED: 4 December 1939: *Regular pass*. 5 March 1951: Stafford Common (Air Ministry sidings)–Bromshall Junction closed completely. December 1952: Stafford–Air Ministry sidings: special services ceased. 19 November 1973: Stafford–Stafford Common closed completely.

REMAINS: *Stafford*: A5013 overbridge and trackbed east of A34 overbridge. *Weston*: Site of S & U bridge over Stone–Colwich line and low embankment to east (984267).

Chartley–Grindley: trackbed traceable.

USES: *Stafford*: council planning to use trackbed for relief road. *Hopton*: cutting in-filled with spoil from A51 improvement and refuse (940265). *Salt*: stationmaster's house in private occupation (958278). Houses on trackbed. *Weston*: trackbed immediately west of Stone–Colwich main line now farmland (980268). Railway bridge across A51 demolished and road alignment improved. Ingestre station was immediately west of A51 (978267). *Grindley*: cutting partly in-filled (044300).

Bibliography

Other people's books have given me a lot of pleasure, as well as information, and it is pleasant to note that this list is not by any means exhaustive of the literature on the railways of the West Midlands. It does not include books mentioned in the text. A fuller bibliography is included in my volume on the West Midlands in the Regional History of the Railways of Great Britain series (David & Charles, volume 7).

From a host of periodicals including the *Railway Magazine* and *Railway World* and the journals of several organisations including the Branch Line Society, the Railway & Canal Historical Society, and the Railway Correspondence & Travel Society, I gleaned, often with sadness, the latest information about trackbed disappearance and development, especially in urban areas, where land is at a premium.

Almost indispensable to research were large-scale road maps dating from the days when they showed railways (and stations) as well as roads. They solved many a puzzle as to where a railway could possibly once have run.

Other old maps, notably Ordnance Survey, also showed where trains once ran, and where their stations were situated, sometimes a mile or more from the places on their nameboards. Official Railway Clearing House maps are invaluable, although their extraneous information is limited. I have enjoyed consulting at the slightest excuse, or without any, that of Staffordshire & District. I bought my 1918 edition from the *Erlestoke Manor* Fund coach at Bewdley station, and that gave added pleasure to a trip along the Severn Valley on an unforgettably beautiful October day when the woods and fields were at their most wistful.

Background Books

Biddle, G. and Nock, O. S., *The Railway Heritage of Britain* (Michael Joseph, 1983)

Birmingham Reference Library, Special collections of railway material.

British Railways Board, *The Reshaping of British Railways* (HMSO, 1963)

Chester-Browne, R., *The Other Sixty Miles: A survey of the abandoned canals of Birmingham and the Black Country* (Birmingham Canal Navigations Society, 1981)

Clinker, C. R., *Railways of the West Midlands: A Chronology 1808–1954* (Stephenson Locomotive Society)

Cooke, R. A., *Track Layout Diagrams: West Midlands GWR & BR*

Daniels, G. and Dench, L. A., *Passengers No More* (Ian Allan)

Hawkins, C. and Reeve, G. *LMS Engine Sheds*, Vol 1 (Wild Swan Publications, 1981)

Hill, N. J. and McDougall, A. O., *A Guide to Closed Railway Lines in Britain 1948–75* (Branch Line Society)

Lambert, A. J., *West Midlands Branch Line Album* (Ian Allan, 1978)

Lewthwaite, G. C., *Branch Line Index* (Branch Line Society)

Lyons, E., *An Historical Survey of Great Western Engine Sheds 1947* (Oxford Publishing Company, 1972)

Lyons, E. and Mountford, E. R., *An Historical Survey of Great Western Engine Sheds 1837–1947* (Oxford Publishing Company, 1979)

MacDermot, E. T., *History of the Great Western Railway* (Ian Allan, 1964)

Price, J. H., *Tramcar, Carriage and Wagon Builders of Birmingham* (Nemo Productions, 1982)

Railway Clearing House, *Railway Junction Diagrams 1915* (David & Charles, 1969)

Thorold, H. *Staffordshire: A Shell Guide* (Faber & Faber, 1982)

Whitehouse, P. B., *The LMS in the West Midlands* (Oxford Publishing Company, 1984)

Chapter 2—Birmingham: GWR

Hadfield, C. and Norris, J., *Waterways to Stratford* (David & Charles, 2nd ed., 1971)

Harrison, D., *Salute to Snow Hill* (Barbryn Press, 1978)

SAVE, *Saving Railway Architecture: Off the Rails* (Save Britain's Heritage, 1977)

Chapter 3—Birmingham: LNWR

Glover, J., *West Midlands Rails in the 1980s* (Ian Allan, 1984)

Chapter 4—Wolverhampton

Dewey, S. and Williams, N., *Wolverhampton Railway Album*, Volumes 1 and 2 (Uralia Press, 1978 and 1983)

Gale, W. K. V. and Hoskison, T. M., *A History of the Pensnett Railway* (The Cottage Press, Codsall, 1969)

Holcroft, H., *The Armstrongs of the Great Western* (Railway World Ltd, 1953)

Jones, G. L. *Railway Walks: Exploring Disused Railways* (David & Charles, 1984)

Wolverhampton Borough Council, *Official Handbook*

Chapter 5—Black Country: GWR

Dudley Borough Council, *Official Guide* (1972–74)

Hale, M. and Williams, N., *By Rail to Halesowen* (Michael Hale and the Uralia Press, 1974)

Halesowen Borough Council, *Official Guide* (1955)

Rowley Regis Borough Council, *Official Guide*, 5th edition.

Williams, N., *Railways of the Black Country, Volume 1: The Byways* (Uralia Press, 1984)

Chapter 6—Black Country: LNWR

Millward, R. and Robinson, A., *The Black Country* (Macmillan, 1971)

Chapter 7—Coventry, Rugby, Leamington Spa

Preston Hendry, Dr R. and Powell Hendry, R., *An Historical Survey of Selected LMS Stations, Layouts and Illustrations* (Oxford Publishing Company, 1982)

Chapter 8—The Midland Presence

Clinker, C. R., *The Birmingham and Derby Junction Railway* (Dugdale Society, 1956)

Chapter 9—North Staffordshire

Christiansen, R. and Miller, R. W., *The North Staffordshire Railway* (David & Charles, 1971)
Hollick, Dr J. R., *The Workings of the Locomotives and Trains of Private Firms over the North Staffordshire Railway* (Private paper)
Jones, P., *The Stafford & Uttoxeter Railway* (The Oakwood Press, 1981)
Lester, C. R., *The Stoke to Market Drayton Line and Associated Canals and Mineral Branches* (The Oakwood Press, 1983)
Somerville, C., *Walking Old Railways* (David & Charles, 1979)
Keys, R. and the North Staffordshire Railway Society, *The Churnet Valley Railway* (1974)

Quotations from *The Loop Line Greenway* are reproduced by kind permission of the City of Stoke-on-Trent.

Acknowledgements

Without the sustained, detailed and enthusiastic help of other people, this book would not have been written. I am especially grateful to three experts who read the manuscript, or part of it: Geoffrey Bannister; Dr J. R. Hollick; and Peter Robinson, Director of the Birmingham Museum of Science and Industry. I have greatly appreciated the help of the City of Birmingham Planning Department, the City Planning Office of Stoke-on-Trent, the West Midlands County Planning Department, and the Staffordshire Moorlands District Council Planning Department; and of Gordon Biddle, Hilary and Maurice Blencowe, R. H. Darlaston, J. Edgington, Harold Forster MBE, R. W. (Bob) Miller, my co-author of the Cambrian Railways and North Staffordshire histories; M. R. C. Price, and, not least, my wife Hilary, who has proofread and been helpful in so many ways.

The sources of the photographs—permission to use which is gratefully acknowledged—will be found in the List of Plates.

Whitefield, Manchester
1985

Index

See also the detailed references to places, branches and associated lines in the Gazetteer. Illustrations are indicated in *italic* type. North Staffordshire places and branches will be found under 'North Staffordshire Railway'.